Praise for *Who Really Cares*

"Breaks new ground... In *Who Really Cares*, Arthur C. Brooks finds that religious conservatives are far more charitable than secular liberals, and that those who support the idea that government should redistribute income are among the least likely to dig into their own wallets to help others." —*Chronicle of Philanthropy*

"This is a thoughtful look at why Americans give and what can be done to encourage giving. Anyone interested in American charities will learn a great deal from Arthur C. Brooks's important book." —*Weekly Standard*

"Provocative... It's not just that charity helps those on the receiving end, says Brooks, an economist at Syracuse University in New York. It also strengthens the cohesion of society at large. Moreover, it appears to make the givers themselves more successful, possibly because the activity transforms them somewhat into better or happier people. Whatever the reasons, he finds that higher income tends to push up charity—and that greater charity tends to push up income." —*Christian Science Monitor*

"Eye-opening... Brooks crunched available data on U.S. charity and found, to his surprise, that conservatives are far more generous than liberals in donating money, time, and even blood. Politics aside, he discovered that, on average, Americans who spurn religion are 'dramatically less likely' to donate than religiously active citizens, whether conservative or liberal."

—*Associated Press*

"James Q. Wilson has called Brooks's book the best study of charitable giving he's ever read, and I would agree wholeheart—"
— ANDREW F

"A clear and well argued book... E
reasoned."

"Syracuse University professor Arthu
become the darling of the religious rig̲... ...merica... In *Who*

Really Cares he cites extensive data analysis to demonstrate that values advocated by conservatives—from church attendance and two-parent families to the Protestant work ethic and a distaste for government-funded social services—make conservatives more generous than liberals." —*Religion News Service*

"Virtue is its own reward—and you will be punished for lack of it. That is the lesson of Arthur Brooks's study of the virtue of charity, a remarkable work of practical philosophy in the plain guise of economics. He has stern words, based on quantitative proof, for liberals who boast of compassion for others but never actually give to them."

—HARVEY MANSFIELD, William R. Kenan, Jr. Professor of Government, Harvard University

"This remarkable book documents the dramatic gap between those who talk about caring and those who actually care. The shattering of stereotypes will be as upsetting to some Americans as it will be encouraging to others."

—FATHER RICHARD JOHN NEUHAUS, editor-in-chief of *First Things*

"Promises to be a highly controversial book…"

—*Raleigh News-Observer*

"Provocative…" —*The Globe and Mail* (Canada)

"This is a book everybody should read—*Who Really Cares* by Arthur Brooks. It's a tremendous book." —PAT ROBERTSON

"A wonderful message for this holiday season." —BRIT HUME

"So what are we to make of the fact that conservative Americans donate 30 percent more to charity than liberal Americans? A new book called *Who Really Cares*, by Syracuse University professor Arthur Brooks, is not going to please the Howard Dean crowd. The book states flat out that religious Americans who vote Republican are far more likely to be generous to the downtrodden than secular-progressives." —BILL O'REILLY

WHO REALLY CARES

WHO REALLY CARES

The Surprising Truth About Compassionate Conservatism

America's Charity Divide—
Who Gives, Who Doesn't,
and Why It Matters

Arthur C. Brooks

Foreword by James Q. Wilson

BASIC
BOOKS

A Member of the Perseus Books Group
New York

Books published by Basic Books are available at special discounts for bulk purchases
in the United States by corporations, institutions, and other organizations. For
more information, please contact the Special Markets Department at the Perseus
Books Group, 2300 Chestnut Street, Suite 200, Philadelphia, PA 19103, or call
(800) 255-1514, or e-mail special.markets@perseusbooks.com.

The Library of Congress has catalogued the hardcover as follows:
Brooks, Arthur C., 1964-
Who really cares : the surprising truth about compassionate conversatism /
Arthur C. Brooks ; foreword by James Q. Wilson.
p. cm.
Includes bibliographical references and index.
ISBN-13: 978-0-465-00821-6 (hardcover : alk. paper)
ISBN-10: 0-465-00821-6 (hardcover : alk. paper)
1. Charities—United States.
2. Voluntarism—United States. 3. Liberals—Charitable contributions—United
States. 4. Conservatives—Charitable contributions—United States. 5. Charity—
Political aspects. I. Title.
HV91.B697 2006
361.7'40973—dc22
2006022485

Paperback: ISBN-13: 978-0-465-00823-0; ISBN-10: 0-465-00823-2

10 9 8 7 6 5 4 3 2 1

To Ester

And now abideth faith, hope, charity, these three; but the greatest of these is charity.

—1 CORINTHIANS 13:13

Contents

Foreword

JAMES Q. WILSON

Nations differ in their history, politics, economics, and culture. Although the first three of these differences have been carefully described and explained by scholars, hardly anyone has done a thorough job of explaining culture.

Yet every person who travels overseas sees and feels the cultural differences immediately. In fact, the tourist senses cultural differences before they learn much about politics and economics. We can read books to learn the history, government, and productive system of France, Italy, or Japan, but we immediately and directly observe that the French, the Italians, and the Japanese behave differently from Americans and from each other.

In this book, Arthur Brooks has found a way to show one aspect of culture: how much time and money people give to charitable causes. Brooks is a rigorously trained scholar (it is very hard to get a PhD from the Rand Graduate School) who can combine careful studies of charity with a direct and compelling way of explaining what he has learned.

Some people may suppose that we cannot learn much about culture from studying charitable giving because how much we give will be dictated by our desire to avoid taxes. And since nations differ in their tax rates, they will no doubt differ in their charitable practices. But this view is a mistake. First, it ignores differences in how much time and effort people donate to other causes. People cannot deduct from their tax bills the labor they donate to philanthropic programs.

Second, about two thirds of all Americans do not deduct any charitable gifts from their tax forms because they take the standard deduction. People who cannot, because of the law, itemize charitable gifts still donate very large sums of money. They cannot do this to avoid taxes.

Third, there does not appear to be any connection between changes in tax rates and how much money people give away. In 1986, the top tax rate was sharply cut. Some people said this was a mistake because charitable gifts would dry up. They did not. In 2001, estate taxes were reduced. Charitable giving was not affected. One reason is that people give away more money when they have more money. Tax rates may have some effect, but not the decisive one.

There are other, more important reasons that explain charity. Religion is one: Religious people donate more money than nonreligious ones, even to secular causes. And since America is a more religious nation than are most European democracies, charitable giving here occurs at a higher rate. There are other causes as well. Brooks finds that what people donate is affected by what they believe about the obligation of the government to reduce income inequality and whether they are part of an intact family.

In short, a careful examination of charity tells us a lot about a nation's culture. And Brooks suggests that charity may also be linked to the economy. It is obvious that affluent people give away more money than poor ones. This may just show that you can only give away money that you already have. But Brooks suggests a different and more fascinating possibility: It may be that charitable giving helps improve the economy. The link may be that charitable habits promote happiness and personal confidence and are associated with the development of good character in one's children.

This book, therefore, is not just about how we contribute time and money; it is also about how our culture may affect our politics and our economy. It is the best study of charity that I have read, and I think you will think that as well.

INTRODUCTION

Charity and Selfishness in America

Are Americans charitable? Many people—including many Americans—would say we are not. Again and again, we are told that America is selfish when it comes to those less fortunate. In 2004, former president Jimmy Carter claimed that Americans are indifferent to suffering around the world: "The problem lies among the people of the U.S. It's a different world from ours. And we don't really care about what happens to them."[1]

Ironically, foreigners are often less likely than Americans to hold such views. Recently, a foreign businessman came to see me at my university office. He told me he wanted to come to the United States to study charity. He had always admired the philanthropic zeal of Americans, and considered it the secret to our success. He had leadership ambitions, and felt it was his duty to become better informed about giving and volunteering so that he could work to encourage these behaviors in his own country.

My guest's impression is nothing new. Another foreign visitor to America famously had the same reaction to American society some 170 years ago. When Alexis de Tocqueville visited the

United States in 1835, he found a spirit of voluntarism and charity unlike anything he had encountered before. In his classic book *Democracy in America,* Tocqueville marveled at America's many civic associations, which were supported through voluntary gifts of time and money: "Americans of all ages, all conditions, and all dispositions constantly form associations," Tocqueville reported. "The Americans make associations to give entertainments, to found seminaries, to build inns, to construct churches, to diffuse books, to send missionaries to the antipodes; in this manner they found hospitals, prisons, and schools."[2]

Who is correct about American charity—Alexis de Tocqueville, or Jimmy Carter? To a certain extent, they're *both* right. When it comes to charity, America is two nations—one charitable, and the other uncharitable. Most Americans are generous, compassionate people. However, there is also an identifiable slice of the population that does not donate to people in need; does not volunteer; does not give in informal ways; does not even feel compassion toward others.

This book is about these two Americas and the reasons they behave so differently. In the process of investigating the forces of charity and selfishness, I have uncovered some hard truths about American culture, politics, and economics. I myself was surprised and disturbed by many of the facts and trends that emerged in the course of my research, and I suspect you will be too.

The stakes are higher than just showing a few surprising truths, however. It matters a lot that we are two nations. Charity, I will show, is essential to our health and happiness, community vitality, national prosperity, and even to our ability to govern ourselves as a free people. I will explain how America's greatest glory lies ahead—if we become more charitable. But I will also offer a warning: Just as America the Charitable spills abundance over

onto the rest of us, America the Selfish threatens ⟍
as a nation through the policies it supports and
encourages.

It is in all our interests to figure out what makes people ⟍⟍
itable, and what makes them uncharitable. Our strength as a nation is affected by our ability to bring more people into the ranks
of the generous—for their good and for ours.

⟋⟍⟋

Fortunately, Tocqueville's America is bigger than Jimmy Carter's:
There are far more charitable Americans than uncharitable ones.
A large majority of U.S. citizens give money away: Approximately three out of four families make charitable donations each
year. The average amount given by these families is $1,800, or
about 3.5 percent of household income. And contrary to what
one might think, it is not true that American giving goes all—or
even mostly—to churches. About a third of individual gifts go
toward religious activities, such as support for houses of worship.
The rest goes to secular activities, such as education, health, and
social welfare. All together, private charitable donations in the
United States add up to about a quarter trillion dollars per year.
Three quarters of this amount comes from private individuals (as
opposed to foundations, corporations, and bequests). To put this
dollar figure into perspective, consider this: Private American
giving could more than finance the entire annual gross domestic
product (GDP) of Sweden, Norway, or Denmark.[3]

Charitable contributions in the United States over the past
fifty years have always been between 1.5 and 2 percent of GDP,
and average giving per household has nearly tripled in inflation-
adjusted dollars over the past half-century. Even though much

popular thought about giving sees a decline in generosity, the truth is that Americans have consistently shared a significant portion of their growing prosperity with charities and churches. [4]

American charity doesn't stop with money. More than half of American families volunteer their time each year. About 40 percent of volunteer hours go to religious causes, followed by about 30 percent for youth-related activities, such as the PTA and children's sports. Poverty-related causes, health charities, and political activism causes also receive significant amounts of volunteer time.[5]

These statistics are impressive, and they belie most of the claims about the selfishness of our nation. That said, an identifiable and sizeable minority of Americans are *not* charitable. Although 225 million Americans give away money each year, the other 75 million *never* give to any causes, charities, or churches. Further, 130 million Americans never volunteer their time.

But are nongivers *really* uncharitable, compared with givers? Maybe most of the people who say they give and volunteer give only a tiny amount. For example, if I give $5 a year, it would technically put me among the "donors"—but it hardly makes me a more charitable person than someone who gives nothing.

But a very bright line exists between people who give and people who don't give. People who *do* give time and money tend to give a lot of it. For example, the percentage of givers donating less than $50 to charity in 2000 was the same as the percentage giving more than $5,000. Similarly, the same percentage of volunteers who volunteered only once volunteered on thirty-six or more occasions in 2000. Twenty percent of volunteers do so at least once a week, and in 2003, this top 20 percent donated an average of three hundred hours of their time.[6]

But mightn't people who don't give or volunteer formally do so informally? Might people who don't send a check to the United Way be more likely than others to help out a family member in need? Or might someone who never volunteers at a soup kitchen be especially likely to give a quarter or a sandwich to a homeless man on the street? It would be ridiculous to label someone as "selfish" just because he or she doesn't make formal charitable donations. Right?

Wrong. People who give away their time and money to established charities are far more likely than nongivers to behave generously in informal ways as well. If we consider all forms of generosity, the difference between charitable and selfish people *grows.* For example, one nationwide survey from 2002 tells us that money donors are nearly three times as likely as nondonors to give money informally to friends and strangers. People who give to charity at least once per year are twice as likely to donate blood as people who don't give money. They are also significantly more likely to give food or money to a homeless person, or to give up their seats to older people on a crowded bus. They are more honest, too: Givers are half again as likely as nongivers to return change mistakenly given to them by a cashier.[7]

Givers are also more sympathetic and tolerant than nongivers. Consider the ways in which donors and nondonors differ in the feelings they express for certain groups in the population. Data from 2002 tell us that givers express less negative prejudice than nongivers toward African Americans, whites, Latinos, and Asians. But it doesn't stop there—they are more sympathetic to Protestants, Jews, Christian fundamentalists, and Catholics. They like labor unions more, but big business more, too; also environmentalists, feminists, welfare recipients, and political conservatives. They like the Supreme Court, Congress, the U.S. military, and the federal government more. Givers are more favorably disposed to everybody than are nongivers. (Everybody, that is, except for two groups: Nongivers like political liberals and the news media slightly more than givers do.)[8]

Although formal charity does not represent all types of generosity, it is an excellent way to flag the people who are truly charitable in American society—and those who are not.

Before talking more about charity, we should define it with a bit more precision. "Charity" comes from the Latin *caritas,* meaning "affection." Scholars go to great pains to distinguish charity from other concepts of giving, such as philanthropy (from the Greek, for "love of man"), and categorize giving with different sorts of motives—from altruism, to religious duty, to social prestige. But in common usage, "charity" encompasses all these things as long as they involve a personal voluntary sacrifice for the good of another person (as well as, perhaps, the good of the giver).

I define "charity" very broadly. Charity can be monetary or it can be nonmonetary—gifts might be of time, or even blood. Charity can be religious or secular, depending on the beliefs and tastes of the giver. It can be formal, such as a check written to the Red Cross, or informal, such as babysitting for a neighbor in need.

I use such an expansive definition of charity because I don't want to leave anything out. The restrictions I do insist on, however, are that charity has to be consensual and beneficial. Were it not so—should the giver or receiver be forced or harmed—an exchange would be either involuntary or unbeneficial and thus hardly an expression of "affection." It is these voluntary, benefi-

Nance

cial, "affectionate" acts that have the ability to transform the giver and receiver in unique and important ways.

Perhaps it helps to think of charity, as I define it, in the following way: Imagine I meet a man with no home. If he forces his way into my home against my will, this is *trespassing*. If I force him to stay with me against his will, this is *kidnapping*. But if I invite him to sleep at my house and he accepts, this is *charity*. This simple definition excludes lots of acts and policies—such as the incarceration of the criminally insane and the taxation of citizens to pay for public services. These might be very wise and proper things to do. But they aren't charity.

How can we explain why some people are charitable, and others selfish? We could ask people to tell us themselves, and many researchers have done so.

In 2000, the main reason people offered for donating to charity was a sense of duty: About 80 percent of givers reported that they gave because "those who have more should give to those who have less." Other common reasons for giving included feeling that the giver owed something to his or her community; because of religious obligation or belief; and simply because of being asked to give. Contrary to what cynics might believe, relatively few givers (only 20 percent) said they gave to get a tax deduction. When it comes to giving time, 96 percent of volunteers in 2000 said one of their motivations was "feeling compassion toward other people." Other frequent reasons included giving back to one's community, and volunteering because it was important to someone the volunteer cared about.[9]

So why *don't* people give? Among those that did not donate any money in 2000, two-thirds said that they could not afford to.

Sense 2 duty

Smaller percentages said it was because nobody asked them, or that they feared the money would be used inefficiently. Among the people who did not volunteer, the most common answer was that they had no time (55 percent). Twenty-eight percent said they were physically unable to do so. Others said they were never asked.[10]

Some of these excuses are almost laughable. It is hard to imagine never being asked to make a donation during an entire year—think how many fund-raising letters you receive every week in the mail. But 4 million Americans claim that this is their experience. And are 46 million Americans (about one in six people) truly physically unable to do anything—anything unpaid, that is—for anybody else?

On the other hand, "not being able to afford to give" certainly sounds like a reasonable excuse. People who don't have money will presumably have a hard time giving it away. But this is not the problem: The working poor in America give more of their money—not less—to charity than middle class people. Indeed, not being able to afford to give is more typically an *upper-income* excuse: Among the people with above-average incomes who did not give charitably in 2000, a majority said that they didn't have enough money. And they probably believed it. We live in a country in which three out of five families carry balances on their credit cards from month to month, and the average household debt for consumer items is about $18,000 (approximately half of which is credit card debt).[11]

I know a couple that fits the "impoverished rich" profile nicely. Cultured, highly educated people, they have a tidy combined income of more than $150,000 per year. But life is expensive: They have a large mortgage, car loans, and kids in college. When all is said and done, there is simply nothing left to give to charity—they "can't afford to give."[12]

One would not have obvious reason to suspect that this couple does not give to charity. And this is the problem with using people's own explanations for why they give or not. People's stated reasons for giving and not giving don't help us predict who is charitable and who is not. However interesting, the reasons people offer don't get us very far in our search for the true differences between generous and selfish people.

So maybe instead of asking people, we should *look* at them. Are there any physical characteristics that stand out to differentiate charitable and selfish people? Can we spot generous and stingy people on the street?

Yes and no. Race and ethnicity, for example, are *not* useful predictors of charity and selfishness. Indeed, American whites and blacks do not give and volunteer at significantly different rates when race is studied in isolation from other characteristics (such as education, income, and religion). But there are other traits, such as age and sex, that are strong predictors of giving. For instance, in 2002, a woman older than thirty was about 18 percentage points more likely than the population average to give. By the same token, a man younger than thirty was far less likely than average to give. This is hardly surprising. Young men are more likely to engage in *every* sort of antisocial behavior in society, from violent crime to drug abuse to—as we now see—basic selfishness. And, more important, this fact does not explain anything about broader patterns of giving. Young males represent less than 10 percent of the population—they are certainly not the only ones not giving.[13]

Ultimately, innate characteristics such as sex and age don't get us much of anywhere in our understanding of the causes of charitable giving. And why should they? My sex and age are not the *reasons* I give and volunteer (or fail to do so). Rather, these characteristics are just associated with the beliefs and behaviors that really do affect my giving. Beliefs and behaviors—this is where the real action is when it comes to charity, and they are the subjects of this book.[14]

—

In the coming chapters, I will explain why people give and why people don't. My explanations are based entirely on data. They are the fruit of years of analysis on the best national and international datasets available on charity, lots of computational horsepower, and the past work of dozens of scholars who have looked at various bits and pieces of the giving puzzle. My objective is to discover the *facts* about charity—whether they happen to conform to preconceived notions or not—as revealed by the evidence. I consider it my job to examine the data, crunch numbers, interpret results, read statistics critically and accurately, *never* to substitute anecdotes for evidence, and to tell you a true story.

This story has some sharp elbows, culturally and politically. Here are a couple of examples.

First, imagine two people: One goes to church every week and strongly rejects the idea that it is the government's responsibility to redistribute income between people who have a lot of money and people who don't. The other person never attends a house of worship, and strongly believes that the government *should* reduce income differences. Knowing only these things, the data tell us that the first person will be roughly twice as likely as the second to give money to charities in a given year, and will give away more than *one hundred times* as much money per year (as well as fifty times more to explicitly nonreligious causes).[15]

Or take two other people who are identical with respect to their household incomes, education, age, sex, and race. One receives assistance from the government in the form of housing support, welfare payments, or food stamps; does not belong to a house of worship; and is a single parent. The second is a working poor person (although his or her total household income is just as low as the first person's, he or she does not receive government assistance), belongs to a house of worship, and is a married parent. According to the data, the second person will be, on average, more than *seven times as likely* to make a donation to charity each year.[16]

As these examples imply with their emphasis on faith, government, and parenthood, the evidence on giving might lead one to the conclusion that culturally traditional people—maybe even political conservatives—are the biggest givers in America today. And the data indicate that political conservatives are, on average, more personally charitable than liberals.* A startling conclusion to be sure—but that's not the end of the story. Conservatives aren't more charitable than liberals simply because their politics somehow make them inherently virtuous—it's far more complicated than that. The *worldview* and *lifestyle* of charitable people are usually just more in sync with the right than they are with the left.

This book shows that four forces in modern American life are primarily responsible for making people charitable. These forces are religion, skepticism about the government in economic life, strong families, and personal entrepreneurism. It is not true that these forces are *exclusive* to the political right, and even less true that they are exclusive to the American Republican Party. Many

---

* Throughout this book, I use the word "liberal" in the modern American, political sense: a person with a left-wing political ideology.

liberals are religious and have rock-solid families—and give a lot. (I grew up in an intact, religious, politically liberal family where giving was important.) But I am talking here about averages, not special cases. It is simply undeniable that today, conservative principles are most congenial to the four forces of charity. Even more, it is obvious that America's political left has increasingly developed a reverse polarity to these forces. As a result, it is fairly natural and instinctive for most political conservatives to behave charitably. Meanwhile, people deeply embedded on the political left are usually not part of a "culture" of giving.

These are not the sorts of conclusions I ever thought I would reach when I started looking at charitable giving in graduate school, ten years ago. I have to admit that I probably would have hated what I have to say in this book. I lived in a world largely characterized by the kind of impressionistic stereotyping offered by President Carter at the beginning of this chapter. Do rich people want tax cuts? I would have told you it's because they are uncharitable. Europeans care more than Americans about the world's poor. Socialism is more compassionate than capitalism. And so on. My personal views about "charity" amounted to little more than unquestioned liberal political beliefs.

When I started doing research on charity, I expected to find that political liberals—who, I believed, genuinely *cared* more about others than conservatives did—would turn out to be the most privately charitable people. So when my early findings led to the opposite conclusion, I assumed I had made some sort of technical error. I re-ran analyses. I got new data. Nothing worked. In the end, I had no option but to change my views.

I confess the prejudices of my past here to emphasize that the findings in this book—many of which may appear conservative and support a religious, hardworking, family-oriented lifestyle—

are faithful to the best available evidence, and *contrary* to my political and cultural roots. Indeed, the irresistible pull of empirical evidence in this book is what changed the way I see the world. It has also guided me in my personal search for the truth—not only as a teacher and researcher but also in my private life as a donor and volunteer, as a father, as a skeptical political independent, and even as a Christian. You'll see why.

I know that some of my conclusions will be controversial, but that is not my purpose now, nor was it my purpose when I began this book. This book does not seek to bash all liberal causes (many of which I support), nor to promote some broad-based political agenda. Rather, the purpose here is to make the point that charity matters, and that we need to understand better what stimulates it. Charity is more than a pleasant personal characteristic, like naturally curly hair or a good singing voice. The evidence I have uncovered has convinced me that charity is important to our personal prosperity, happiness, health, and ability to express ourselves humanely. Furthermore, the policies, politics, and cultural forces that compromise the willingness and ability of people to give charitably induce a personal flaw into citizens that impoverishes them, stunts their opportunities, and has negative repercussions for our communities, our politics, and our nation. Those are the stakes, and they are the reason I wrote this book.

CHAPTER 1

Is Compassionate Conservatism an Oxymoron?

We are the Folk Song Army,
Every one of us cares.
We all hate poverty, war and injustice,
Unlike the rest of you squares.
Tom Lehrer, *"The Folk Song Army"*[1]

Like most universities, mine is flanked by a neighborhood where a lot of students and faculty live. I walk through this neighborhood each day on my way to work. It is pleasant and relatively quiet, but far from homogeneous. The diversity of race, ethnicity, and religion is one of the reasons the university neighborhood is an interesting place.

But one way in which the neighborhood is not at all diverse is politics. Liberal political views are far more common here than they are in the general population, and this was never more obvious than during the run-up to the 2004 presidential election. The normally mellow neighborhood took on a hard edge as political bumper stickers and yard signs popped up everywhere. "Regime Change Starts at Home," read one sign, overtly comparing President George W. Bush to the Iraqi dictator Saddam Hussein, who had recently been ousted by American forces under a policy dubbed "regime change." In a display of patriotic irony another exhorted: "Defend America: Defeat Bush." By far the most common sign around town, however, was produced by a local liberal activist group. It bore the unironic slogan, "Bush Must Go! Human Need, Not Corporate Greed."

Strident political messages are fairly unremarkable in this—or any other—university neighborhood, but one fact made these striking: New York State was uncompetitive in the 2004 election. John F. Kerry, the Democratic challenger, had led Mr. Bush by wide margins since the beginning of the campaign, and he took the state-wide election by 19 percentage points—more than a million votes. In other words, the neighbors were vigorously campaigning in what amounted to an uncontested election.

It was as if the campaigning had a purpose unrelated to the election. After all, "Human Need, Not Corporate Greed" is unlikely to win over many Republican voters. It is difficult to imagine some lost political conservative happening into the university neighborhood and, upon reading the slogans, undergoing a sudden conversion: "It's true! Human need *is* more important than corporate greed—I don't know why I never realized it before!" The real function of the signs, I believe, was to display the virtuousness of the bearers while lambasting the selfishness of President Bush and his supporters. The signs were just one more opportunity to reinforce the stereotypes of conservative selfishness and liberal generosity.

These are, perhaps, the most common stereotypes in our modern American political discourse: The political left is compassionate and charitable toward the less fortunate, but the political right is oblivious to suffering. As I have already confessed, this stereotype once characterized my own beliefs. If you had asked me a few years ago to sum up the character of American conservatives, I would have said they were hard-headed pragmatists who were willing to throw your grandmother out into the snow to preserve some weird ideal of self-reliance. Hardworking, perhaps—but certainly not generous. In contrast, I would have told you that even though some liberal sentiments and policies were ill-conceived, they generally emanated from a fundamental sense of compassion and charity toward others.

These stereotypes are common not just among the politically uninformed; plenty of experts adhere to this worldview as well. For example, the noted linguistics scholar George Lakoff, author of the bestselling book about political discourse *Don't Think of an Elephant: Know Your Values and Frame the Debate,* theorizes: "The conservative moral system . . . has as its highest value preserving and defending the 'strict father' system. . . . Meanwhile, liberals' conceptual system of the 'nurturant parent' has as its highest value helping individuals who need help." That is, charity is a natural by-product of the politically progressive mindset, and it is passed on in liberal families—but not in conservative families.[2]

Some have even argued that conservatism stems from childhood personality problems. In 1969, for example, two psychologists at the University of California at Berkeley evaluated one hundred Berkeley-area preschoolers. Decades later, they asked the subjects about their political opinions. The researchers found that the politically liberal young adults in this group had been the more resourceful, autonomous, expressive, and self-reliant children. In contrast, the young adults that turned into conservatives had been judged as children to be rigid, easily offended, "visibly deviant," and susceptible to guilt feelings. Such findings might appear consistent with a psychological link between liberalism and compassion toward others—as well as a link between conservatism and selfishness.[3]

After the 2004 presidential election, vast regions of the country were dismissed as selfish—because they had voted Republican. An essay published by the online magazine *Slate*, "The Unteachable Ignorance of the Red States," argued that conservative "red state" America is irredeemably uncharitable, but "blue state" communities, which voted in greater part for John Kerry, tend to be good and compassionate and are thus fodder for red-state predators: "The blue state citizens make the Rousseauvian mistake of thinking humans are essentially good, and so they never realize when they are about to be slugged from behind."[4]

Politicians have milked these stereotypes for everything they are worth. General Wesley Clark, a Democratic candidate for president in 2004, stated it succinctly in this attack on George W. Bush: "The only charity [to which Bush has] given is . . . big business and the very rich." Mr. Bush is not the only conservative political leader labeled as personally uncharitable. Nearly twenty years after the end of his presidency, many still vilify Ronald Reagan for his supposed lack of generosity and compassion. Whether or not it is an *ad hominem* substitute for a substantive criticism, it is still common to hear in the mainstream news media, as one prominent newspaper columnist stated, that Reagan was "the most antipoor, antiblack, and antidisadvantaged [president] in the latter half of the 20th century." Shortly after Reagan's death in 2004, the *Baltimore Chronicle* published an article subtly titled "Killer, Coward, Conman: Good Riddance, Gipper!" The author wrote that Reagan's values were "union busting and a declaration of war on the poor and anyone who couldn't buy designer dresses." He added, "It was the New Meanness, bringing starvation back to America so that every millionaire could get another million."[5]

Liberals don't stop at accusing conservatives of simple selfishness—they accuse them of *ungodly* selfishness. In November 2005, John Kerry lambasted conservative policymakers for the way they "give" to some and "take" from others. And he did so in explicitly Christian terms: "There is not anywhere in the three-year ministry of Jesus Christ, anything that remotely suggests—not one miracle, not one parable, not one utterance—that says you ought to cut children's health care or take money from the poorest people in our nation to give it to the wealthiest people in our nation." That is, conservative lawmakers violate the basic premises of Christian charity in proposing cuts to government social welfare spending. In December 2005, Jim Wallis, the liberal Christian writer and political advocate, took this a step further in response to Republican budget cuts to social programs: "[Christian conservatives] are trading the lives of poor people for their [political] agenda. They're being, and this is the worst insult, unbiblical." He went on to quote Isaiah 10:1–2: "Woe unto them that decree unrighteous decrees, and that write grievousness which they have prescribed, to turn aside the needy from judgment, and to take away the right from the poor of my people, that widows may be their prey, and that they may rob the fatherless!"[6]

Liberals are not the only ones who accept the stereotype of conservative selfishness. Some conservatives often embrace it as well. For example, in 2000, George W. Bush, then running for the presidency, used the label "compassionate conservative" to describe his proposed approach to governance. He proposed this as an innovation—as if he were going against the grain of conservative tradition. "Like traditional conservatism," his domestic policy advisor explained, "compassionate conservatism assumes that the marketplace is the best way to deliver value. But compassionate conservatives also recognize that the prosperity created by the marketplace has left many Americans behind and that government has a responsibility to reach out to those who are at the bottom rungs of the economic ladder."[7]

Politicians on both sides cried foul. A Democratic Party spokeswoman asserted, bluntly, that "compassionate conservatism is an oxymoron." But many conservatives rejected the idea as well: Dan Quayle, the former vice president, called the label "silly and insulting," and "code for surrendering our values and principles."[8]

The conventional wisdom runs like this: Liberals are charitable because they advocate government redistribution of money in the name of social justice; conservatives are uncharitable because they oppose these policies. But note the sleight of hand: Government spending, according to this logic, is a form of charity.

Let us be clear: *Government spending is not charity.* It is not a voluntary sacrifice by individuals. No matter how beneficial or humane it might be, no matter how necessary it is for providing public services, it is still the obligatory redistribution of tax revenues. Because government spending is not charity, sanctimonious yard signs do not prove that the bearers are charitable or that their opponents are selfish. (On the contrary, a public attack on the integrity of those who don't share my beliefs might more legitimately constitute evidence that *I* am the uncharitable one.)

To evaluate accurately the charity difference between liberals and conservatives, we must consider private, voluntary charity. How do liberals and conservatives compare in their private giving and volunteering? Beyond strident slogans and sarcastic political caricatures, what, exactly, do the *data* tell us?

The data tell us that the conventional wisdom is dead wrong. In most ways, political conservatives are *not* personally less charitable than political liberals—they are more so.

First, we must define "liberals" and "conservatives." Most surveys ask people not just about their political party affiliation but also about their ideology. In general, about 10 percent of the population classify themselves as "very conservative"; and another 10 percent call themselves "very liberal." About 20 percent say they are simply "liberal," and 30 percent or so say they are "conservative." The remaining 30 percent call themselves "moderates" or "centrists." In this discussion, by "liberals" I mean the approximately 30 percent in the two most liberal categories, and by conservatives I mean the 40 percent or so in the two most conservative categories.

So how do liberals and conservatives compare in their charity? When it comes to giving or not giving, conservatives and liberals look a lot alike. Conservative people are a percentage point or two more likely to give money each year than liberal people, but a percentage point or so less likely to volunteer.[9]

But this similarity fades away when we consider average dollar amounts donated. In 2000, households headed by a conservative gave, on average, 30 percent more money to charity than households headed by a liberal ($1,600 to $1,227). This discrepancy is not simply an artifact of income differences; on the contrary, liberal families earned an average of 6 percent *more* per year than conservative families, and conservative families gave more than liberal families within every income class, from poor to middle class to rich.[10]

If we look at party affiliation instead of ideology, the story remains largely the same. For example, registered Republicans were seven points more likely to give at least once in 2002 than registered Democrats (90 to 83 percent).[11]

The differences go beyond money and time. Take blood donations, for example. In 2002, conservative Americans were more likely to donate blood each year, and did so more often, than liberals. If liberals and moderates gave blood at the same rate as conservatives, the blood supply in the United States would jump by about 45 percent.[12]

The political stereotypes break down even further when we consider age: "Anyone who is not a socialist before age thirty has no heart, but anyone who is still a socialist after thirty has no head," goes the old saying. And so we imagine crusty right-wing grandfathers socking their money away in trust funds while their liberal grandchildren work in soup kitchens and save the whales. But young liberals—perhaps the most vocally dissatisfied political constituency in America today—are one of the least generous demographic groups out there. In 2004, self-described liberals younger than thirty belonged to one-third fewer organizations in their communities than young conservatives. In 2002, they were 12 percent less likely to give money to charities, and one-third less likely to give blood. Liberal young Americans in 2004 were also significantly less likely than the young conservatives to express a willingness to sacrifice for their loved ones: A lower percentage said they would prefer to suffer than let a loved one

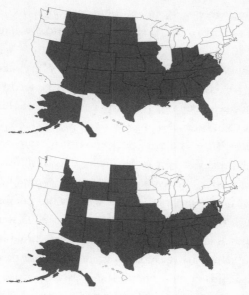

MAP 1.1   Top: Electoral Map (Kerry States in White)
Bottom: Charitable Giving, 2001 (Below-Average States in White)

suffer, that they are not happy unless the loved one is happy, or that they would sacrifice their own wishes for those they love.[13]

The compassion of American conservatives becomes even clearer when we compare the results from the 2004 U.S. presidential election to data on how states address charity. Using Internal Revenue Service data on the percentage of household income given away in each state, we can see that the red states are more charitable than the blue states. For instance, of the twenty-five states that donated a portion of household income above the national average, twenty-four gave a majority of their popular votes to George W. Bush for president; only one gave the election to John F. Kerry. Of the twenty-five states below the national giving average, seventeen went for Kerry, but just seven for Bush. In other words, the electoral map and the charity map are remarkably similar.[14]

These results are not an artifact of close elections in key states. The average percentage of household income donated to charity in each state tracked closely with the percentage of the popular vote it gave to Mr. Bush. Among the states in which 60 percent or more voted for Bush, the average portion of income donated to charity was 3.5 percent. For states giving Mr. Bush less than 40 percent of the vote, the average was 1.9 percent. The average amount given per household from the five states combined that gave Mr. Bush the highest vote percentages in 2003 was 25 percent more than that donated by the average household in the five northeastern states that gave Bush his lowest vote percentages; and the households in these liberal-leaning states earned, on average, 38 percent *more* than those in the five conservative states.[15]

People living in conservative states volunteer more than people in liberal states. In 2003, the residents of the top five "Bush states" were 51 percent more likely to volunteer than those of the bottom five, and they volunteered an average of 12 percent more total hours each year. Residents of these Republican-leaning states volunteered more than twice as much for religious organizations, but also far more for secular causes. For example, they were more than twice as likely to volunteer to help the poor.[16]

Surely Jimmy Carter would have been surprised to learn that the selfish Americans he criticized so vociferously were most likely the very people who elected him president.

These results may surprise you—they certainly surprised me. Many people will object to these conclusions, so let's address some of the counterarguments.

One could argue that my definition of charity is too narrow, and that by focusing only on voluntary giving I have excluded the most significant means by which Americans transfer their assets to the poor: taxes. Certainly, liberals frequently support government social welfare policies that (they believe) improve the lives of many Americans. Indeed, 48 percent of self-described liberals in 2002 said the government spends too little on welfare programs (compared with just 9 percent of conservatives who said this). Isn't support for welfare programs a kind of charity?

I argue that it is not. American liberals and conservatives live together in a democracy, and public policies apply to both groups equally. Liberals usually believe that we spend too little on social welfare programs; conservatives usually believe that we spend too much. Which group is right is beside the point. Our prevailing policies reflect the will of the voters, more or less, and one person's viewpoint will not bend policy much unless it is shared by a sufficient number of fellow citizens. I am not more or less compassionate simply because I support taxing wealthy people, nor if I am dissatisfied with the adequacy of government social programs. Although outrage over the callousness of our public policies toward the poor may produce a sense of moral correctness—and may be justified—it will not relieve anybody's suffering. Worse yet, if moral outrage is only a substitute for private charity, the needy will become *worse* off than before.[17]

One might argue that unless I consider one's giving motives, I will confuse conservative giving with "true" charity. For example, can I really call it "charity" when a Republican investment banker donates money to the Metropolitan Opera because he wants to enhance his social standing? George Bernard Shaw put it this way: "Most of the money given by rich people in 'charity' is made up of conscience money, 'ransom,' political bribery, and bids for titles. . . . One buys moral credit by signing a cheque, which is easier than turning a prayer wheel." In other words, if some—perhaps most—conservative giving isn't really altruistic, maybe we shouldn't count it as charity.[18]

This kind of logic has been invoked in America throughout its history. Andrew Carnegie, the millionaire industrialist and philanthropist of the late nineteenth century (he died in 1919), was criticized for his supposedly uncharitable charity. Carnegie stated in his famous essay "The Gospel of Wealth" that "the man who dies . . . rich dies disgraced." It is ironic that he died very rich. But one cannot say that his "disgrace" was for lack of effort. During his lifetime, Carnegie gave away more than $350 million ($4 billion in today's dollars) for the creation of 2,509 libraries throughout the English-speaking world. Not good enough, in the minds of many. One liberal charity expert dismisses the giving of Carnegie and others as "the conversion of vast amounts of wealth accumulated during America's 'Gilded Age' by conservative, anti-labor, laissez-faire businessmen into 'clean money.'" That is, the sort of giving practiced by Carnegie and is nothing more than a means of expiating the guilt that comes with extreme wealth.[19]

But who knows what motivates anyone? It is an act of rank hubris to dismiss a charitable act on the mere supposition that the motives of the giver are somehow impure. Social scientists have identified a multiplicity of giving motives, including the "warm glow" one feels from giving, the provision of goods for one's own social group (such as a church), guilt, duty, social pressure, or the pursuit of status. And researchers conducting laboratory experiments on human subjects have even found what looks suspiciously like real altruism—giving to others whom they do not know, and will never meet.[20]

Ultimately, however, the giver's motive is irrelevant. Charity depends on behavior, not on motive. Looking for motives leads to the nonsensical argument that someone who gives nothing but supports the *idea* of helping others is more generous than a person who donates to charities and causes but who has no apparent great love for mankind. Although this argument might have theological merit, it is not useful for understanding private generosity and its benefits for society. (And it sounds suspiciously like an excuse not to write a personal check.)

A third argument against the idea that conservatives are actually generous is that much conservative giving doesn't aid "truly needy" people: It mostly goes to churches and upper-crust nonprofits such as universities and symphony orchestras. The political left harbors a common belief that gifts are not really charity if they do not relieve poverty or promote social equality. No better example of this view was on display than in November 2005, when the *New York Times* devoted a special section to "giving." The front page of the section featured a clever graphic in which a cooked fish on a silver platter was being uncovered—but all the flesh was absent and there were only bones. The clear implication was that American giving (undertaken to a large extent by wealthy and religious people—many of whom are conservatives, of course) may look like a feast, but it is nothing of the sort. In the lead article, titled "What Is Charity?" the *Times* reported that American philanthropy was "turning away from Americans most in need of charity." This assertion came about because even though charitable donations in America had increased over the past fifty years, the share of donations going to human service organizations (such as soup kitchens and homeless shelters) had fallen. Larger percentages had gone instead to organizations that allegedly serve donors' interests, such as symphony orchestras, elite hospitals, and religious organizations. This giving, the argument went, was not really charitable because it did not help America's needy.[21]

This argument distorts the facts. First, the explosion in total dollars donated in America has more than made up for a lower percentage given to human services: Even with population growth, the inflation-adjusted, per-capita amount given by Americans to human service charities was 14 percent higher in 2004 than in 1960. Second, over the same period, the percentage of the American population living in poverty fell by half, and the amount of real federal government payments to the poor increased by more than 500 percent. In other words, although there still is need in the United States, it has decreased over the last fifty years—but private charity to alleviate this need has not. Finally, real private giving to all causes in America increased fivefold from 1955 to 2004; this means that more and more of the organizations helping the underprivileged, as well as the rest of us, are funded through private donations. In short, the argument about giving to the wrong causes is factually incorrect (but common nonetheless).[22]

But what if it *were* true that conservative people are giving only to houses of worship and elite nonprofits? Would this make the giving less valid? Certainly, some on the left believe that the object of charitable giving matters crucially. The American political left has, for example, attacked the low-cost retail giant Wal-Mart (founded by Sam Walton) with near-religious zeal of late, scrutinizing and criticizing every part of the company's business practices, including its corporate philanthropy and the giving of Walton's family. In 2005, the National Committee for Responsive Philanthropy (NCRP), a liberal advocacy group, issued a report condemning the company and the family's charitable giving to causes such as school voucher movements and conservative think tanks as a façade for a "conservative political agenda and personal financial gain." According to the report, "the Waltons' and Wal-Mart's philanthropy deserves more scrutiny than praise." The NCRP doesn't believe the Waltons are charitable because it doesn't like the causes they support.

This kind of argument is hopelessly subjective and dangerously arrogant. No doubt most people think *their* causes are better than everyone else's. Conservatives think that donations to the Heritage Foundation are better than those to the American Civil Liberties Union; atheists believe donations to churches are a waste of money (or worse), and so it goes. But it is unwise for individuals or groups to dismiss the sacrifices of other Americans lest their sacrifices be dismissed as well. Every American *should* think about the cause or causes that matter to him or her. And different Americans will come up with different answers. Some will give to soup kitchens, some to the Metropolitan Museum of Art. We should be thankful for these differences, which are the reason Americans support such a broad range of programs, from inner-city renewal to universities to the great museums. Social programs are desperately needed, of course, but symphony orchestras and private universities are important, too. Most Americans would regret the depressing bleakness that would result if every service in culture, education, religion, and research were sacrificed in exchange for wider support for basic human needs.

When it comes to private charity, conservatives have the upper hand over liberals—we know this. It might be tempting to stop here, because this finding so roundly refutes the common political wisdom. However, this isn't the end of the story. Just because conservatives tend to give more than liberals doesn't mean that ideology *causes* this difference. When we hold all personal characteristics constant, people of differing politics are usually not distinguishable by how they give. This means that political ideology by itself does not drive charity differences; rather, the things that go along with political beliefs account for most of the differences we see between ideological groups.

Conservatives and liberals differ in lots of ways, of course. But four lifestyle and worldview differences—described in the next four chapters—explain most of the reasons conservatives are usually more generous than liberals. These reasons are the real story behind the giving differences discussed in this chapter.

So should we care about political differences in charity? Indeed we should, because political ideology is a dominant feature of America's cultural landscape; many people holding strong political opinions might change their attitudes when they are aware of the facts. First, liberals of good will can use the evidence presented here to update their views on giving and stop belittling the charity of their conservative brethren. Second, charitable and potentially charitable liberals might see this information as a call to arms, and give more as a result. Finally, these facts can help to answer the use of charity as a weapon of progressive rhetoric and so strengthen the accuracy and fairness of political debate in America.

CHAPTER 2

FAITH AND CHARITY

To him who ever thought with love of me
Or ever did for my sake some good deed
I will appear, looking such charity
And kind compassion, at his life's last need
That he will out of hand and heartily
Repent he sinned and all his sins be freed.
GERARD MANLEY HOPKINS *(1844–1889)[1]*

Here is a curious fact: Families in San Francisco give almost exactly the same amount to charity each year as families in South Dakota: about $1,300. This may seem counterintuitive, because in every other respect, the two communities—1,500 miles apart—could not be more different. South Dakota spreads the same population as San Francisco County's over an area 1,615 times larger. A South Dakotan is half as likely to hold a college degree as a San Franciscan.[2]

The $1,300 to charity represents a significant difference as well, because the average San Francisco family enjoys 78 percent more personal income than a family in South Dakota. For a family making $45,364 (the South Dakota state average), $1,300 represents a much larger sacrifice than for one making $80,822 (the San Francisco County average). So the real difference in giving between the communities is this: The average South Dakotan family gives away 75 percent more of its household income each year than the average family in San Francisco.[3]

I asked an executive at the South Dakota Community Foundation why South Dakotans donate so much of their incomes to charity. Her response was immediate: religion. "We were all taught to tithe here," she told me, referring to the biblical injunction to believers that they donate 10 percent of their incomes to charity. Further, she explained, even those who do not attend church regularly donate a lot because they were taught to do so by their parents, who probably *did* attend. If people in South Dakota learn charity from religious practice, does a lack of religion explain low charity levels in San Francisco? That is the question I took to the director of a major San Francisco foundation. "Yes," she told me, "this is a pretty godless place. People don't feel very obligated to give." The numbers bear out these claims: Fifty percent of South Dakotans attend their houses of worship every week, versus 14 percent of San Franciscans. On the other hand, 49 percent of San Franciscans never attend church, but the statistic drops to 10 percent for South Dakotans.[4]

The two foundation executives were claiming that religion causes people to behave charitably. If this is right, why is it so— and why does secularism depress giving? Maybe there's less here than meets the eye, and the difference between South Dakotans and San Franciscans amounts to little more than tithing to churches. I asked these questions as I explored the link between religion and charity—and the answers surprised me.

The impact of religion on charity could, in theory, go either way. On the one hand, we might assume that faith creates a positive tendency to behave charitably toward others; after all, people practicing mainstream religions in America are constantly taught to give to others, and even to love their enemies. All major Christian traditions require their adherents to give. In the New Testament, Jesus says, "Give, and it will be given to you. A good measure, pressed down, shaken together and running over, will be poured into your lap. For with the measure you use, it will be measured to you." Similarly, charity (in the form of *zakat*) is the Fourth Pillar of Islam; Judaism commands *tzedaka*—support of a fellow person in need; Tibetan Buddhism teaches that "compassion compels us to reach out to all living beings, including our so-called enemies, those people who upset or hurt us." Hinduism teaches, "Find and follow the good path, ruled by compassion. Of the many ways, that one leads to liberation."[5]

On the other hand, it is also possible that religion could discourage charity—particularly toward groups or programs that fall outside a particular community of faith. Not everyone believes that religion correlates with virtue: Particularly in the wake of the September 11, 2001, terrorist attacks on New York and Washington, D.C., many people articulated the idea that religion—religious zealotry—was to blame for the tragedy. Much wickedness has been done in the name of religion, people remind us, and they point to the Spanish Inquisition five hundred years ago and the Taliban today.

But the evidence leaves no room for doubt: Religious people are far more charitable than nonreligious people. In years of research, I have never found a measurable way in which secularists are more charitable than religious people.

Let's begin by defining what "religious" and "secular" mean. Most surveys ask people how often they attend a house of worship. "Religious people," as I define them here, attend nearly every week or more, and make up about a third of the population. "Secularists" attend infrequently (a couple of times a year) or never—or they say they have no religion. The rest of the American population—a bit over 40 percent, in most surveys—profess a religion and attend sometimes, but not regularly. There are other ways to differentiate religious and secular people, of course. But I will show that, no matter how religion is defined, the same story about charity emerges.

In 2000, 81 percent of one large nationwide survey of Americans said they gave money to charity, and 57 percent said they volunteered. But the likelihood of giving and volunteering was dramatically different between religious people and secularists: Religious people were 25 percentage points more likely to give than secularists (91 to 66 percent). Religious people were also 23 points more likely to volunteer (67 to 44 percent).[6]

Instead of just the decision to give or not, what about the differences in the average dollar amounts of money donated, and amount of time volunteered? This comparison increases the gap between the groups. In 2000, religious people—who, per family, earned exactly the same amount as secular people, $49,000—gave about 3.5 time more money per year (an average of $2,210 versus $642). They also volunteered more than twice as often (12 times per year, versus 5.8 times).

That religious people would give more to religious organizations and charities than secular people is a given, but it does not explain enormous overall charity differences. If a religious person and a secular person were equally generous—but the former gave to a church and the latter to the Red Cross—we should see no difference in *total* giving (especially since religious people do not earn more than secularists). But the giving differences between the groups is undeniable.

These giving differences could be a result of religion itself, or rather of characteristics related to religion, such as (perhaps) race, education, or gender. But it turns out that the nonreligious differences do not explain much of the gap at all: Controlling for these differences, an enormous charity gap still remains between religious people and secular people. To see this, imagine two women who are both forty-five years old, white, married, have an annual household income of $50,000, and attended about a year of college. The only difference between them is that one goes to church every week, but the other never does. The churchgoing woman will be 21 percentage points more likely to make a charitable gift of money during the year than the nonchurchgoer, and will also be 26 points more likely to volunteer. Furthermore, she will tend to give $1,383 more per year to charity, and to volunteer on 6.4 more occasions.[7]

Religion dwarfs all other possible differences between the women in predicting charity. For example, the difference between the religious woman and the secularist in the likelihood of giving money is seven times greater than the difference between a fifty-year-old and a twenty-year-old. It is also higher than the difference between a college graduate and a high school dropout. Religious differences also swamp political differences, although, as we shall see, religion and politics *together* make for a potent mix in stimulating charity (or selfishness).

You might suspect that I have defined religion in a way that skews results, since different religions and denominations offer (or require) different levels of attendance for a person to remain in "good standing." For example, a pious Catholic may be a daily communicant, but a reasonably observant Jew might attend services only on High Holy Days and therefore not fulfill my criterion of weekly attendance. And, you might argue, attending a house of worship may not be a particularly religious act: Some people belong to religious communities for social rather than spiritual reasons. And such people might even inflate reports of their own giving to reassure themselves (and others) that they are meeting expectations.[8]

So let's leave attendance out of it for a moment. Let's look at other kinds of religious and spiritual behaviors for the same kind of differences. The results are dramatic: People who pray every day (whether or not they go to church) are 30 percentage points more likely to give money to charity than people who never pray (83 to 53 percent). Simply belonging to a congregation—whether one attends regularly or not—makes a person 32 points more likely to give (88 to 56 percent). And people saying they devote a "great deal of effort" to their spiritual lives are 42 points more likely to give than those devoting "no effort" (88 to 46 percent). Even a belief in *beliefs themselves* is associated with charity: People who say that "beliefs don't matter as long as you're a good person" are dramatically less likely to give charitably (69 to 86 percent) and to volunteer (32 to 51 percent) than people who think that beliefs *do* matter.[9]

These results are not exclusive to particular religious faiths. It doesn't matter much what religion one practices as long as it is practiced seriously. Indeed, among those who attended worship services regularly in 2000, 92 percent of Protestants gave charitably, compared with 91 percent of Catholics, 91 percent of Jews, and 89 percent from other religions.[10]

The differences between religion and secularism are evident in the generosity of particular states and regions. Take Arkansas as an example. Arkansas has about two houses of worship per thousand residents, the fourth highest level in the country. Residents give 3.9 percent of their incomes to charity each year, on average, the fifth highest among the states. Arkansas is typical. Nineteen of the twenty-five states with the most houses of worship per capita in 2000 were also above average in their household giving. This all makes sense, of course: Communities supporting numerous churches tend to give them time and money—which explains why there are so many churches in the first place.[11]

Where does the money go in more secular states? Not very far. Religious charity in the highly churched states is *not* offset in the more secular states by nonreligious giving. Consider Massachusetts, which has just 0.54 houses of worship per thousand residents (forty-eighth in the nation). Its residents give away only 1.8 percent of their incomes to all types of charity each year (the lowest level in the nation). Indeed, nineteen of the twenty-five states with the fewest houses of worship per capita were below the national average in all types of household giving.

We know that politically conservative "red states" tend to give a lot more than liberal "blue states." One philanthropy expert explained this political phenomenon in the same religious terms that the San Francisco foundation executive used in our conversation: "They are tithing, evangelical Protestants, and they are giving in proportion to their income. Up here [in the blue state

Northeast], religion doesn't help our giving. I wouldn't say it hurts, but it doesn't help, either." This assessment—that low religious participation does not help giving—considerably understates the effects of secularism.[12]

The evidence so far is pretty compelling. But I was still left with doubts about comparing the giving of religious and secular people. A lot of smart people believe that religious giving and volunteering are not really charity—they are gifts to something like a club. I disagree with these arguments, but I have to take them seriously, and ask: When we look only at gifts of time and money to explicitly secular causes, how do religious and nonreligious people compare? Are the enormous giving differences wiped out?

Not even close. Religious people are more charitable in every measurable nonreligious way—including secular donations, informal giving, and even acts of kindness and honesty—than secularists.

In 2000, 68 percent of households gave money to charities having no religious affiliation. Fifty-one percent volunteered for secular causes. The average amount of money contributed to completely secular charities per household was $502, about 37 percent of total donations. These figures tell us that American giving is concerned with a lot more than houses of worship and faith-based charities.

But these high nonreligious giving levels were not the same for religious people and secularists. Although the charity gap between these groups was not as wide in secular giving as it was for all types of giving, religious people were still 10 points more likely than secularists to give money to nonreligious charities such as the United Way (71 to 61 percent), and 21 points more likely to volunteer for completely secular causes such as the local

PTA (60 to 39 percent). In addition, the value of the average religious household's donations to nonreligious charities was 14 percent higher than the average secular household's.[13]

Once again, this difference is truly due to religion. Compare two people who are identical in every way except religious participation. The churchgoer will be 9 points more likely than the secularist to give to nonreligious charities, and will give $88 more to these organizations each year. He or she will also be 25 points more likely to volunteer for secular causes.[14]

Financial gifts to and volunteering for secular causes are not the only forms of secular giving. What about gifts of money to family and friends? Here, too, secularists lag behind religious people. For example, data from 2000 on informal giving tell us that people belonging to religious congregations were 8 percent more likely to give money to family and friends than people who did not belong. Furthermore, the value of their informal gifts was, on average, 46 percent higher.[15]

The story is the same even when it comes to informal acts of kindness to others. In 2002, religious people were far more likely to donate blood than secularists, to give food or money to a homeless person, to return change mistakenly given them by a cashier, and to express empathy for less fortunate people. Even if they did engage in informal charitable acts, secularists were less likely to do so frequently. For example, religious people were 57 percent more likely than secularists to help a homeless person at least once a month.[16]

This is not to say that secularists *never* engage in acts of kindness and charity, nor that religious people *always* do. But the data show very large differences between the groups, with results we can witness in our everyday lives. For example, if a cashier gives a churchgoer too much change, the odds are better than half that she will return it, but the odds are more than 6 in 10 that a secularist will *not* give it back. If the workplace has a blood drive and a colleague asks them to donate, the churchgoer is two-thirds more likely to say yes than the secularist. This is evidence that the gap in charity correlates with a broader gap in everyday virtue, and that both are related to religious behavior—or a lack of it.[17]

Let's make the distinction between religious and secular people even more tangible. Consider a major event in the world of American secular charity: the September 11, 2001, terror attacks. Nearly two-thirds of all Americans gave money to 9/11-related causes in the weeks following the tragedy, and more than a quarter gave other gifts (such as blood). It was an astonishing and unprecedented response to a tragedy, and it represented an outpouring of charity across the sociopolitical spectrum in America. Yet even here, religion played a major role: People who never attended church were 11 percentage points less likely than regular churchgoers to give to a 9/11 cause (56 to 67 percent). Even after controlling for personal attributes—age, income, education, gender, race, and family size—secularists were 10 percentage points less likely to give to a 9/11-related cause than religious people.[18]

It is clear that religious people do not outperform secularists in charity simply because of their gifts to houses of worship. Religious people are, inarguably, more charitable in *every measurable way*. Secularists who impugn the charity of religious people by claiming that much of their giving goes "merely" to houses of worship should note that, for a substantial portion of the secular population, religious charity is replaced by . . . nothing. Less than nothing, because secularists are generally less generous in nonreligious ways as well.

Why are secularists so uncharitable? We might start by simply asking them. In doing so, an interesting pattern emerges: Secularist nongivers are far more likely to give excuses for their lack of charity than religious nongivers. Imagine two people who do not give to charity: one secularist, and one churchgoer. The secularist is more than twice as likely as the churchgoer to say it is because he or she was never asked, and more than three times as likely to say he or she couldn't afford to give—even though an average secularist nongiver earns 16 percent *more* money each year than a religious nongiver. Other common excuses among secularists for not giving are that they make contributions only through the workplace ("I gave at the office"), or even that they "do not believe in charity."[19]

The secularist nongiver is also twice as likely to argue that charities "waste donations." This argument is especially common for religious charities, and the point of view goes far beyond some hardcore atheist fringe. The vice president of George Soros's Open Society Institute (an organization that philanthropically supports civil society initiatives around the world), for example, argues that religious charities, funded in no small part by religious givers, are more expensive to run than their secular equivalents: "A program that deals with drug addiction as sinful behavior curable through Bible classes—and much touted by the supporters of faith-based approaches to social problems . . . actually costs more to deliver than conventional drug treatment."[20]

It is probably true that such programs are more expensive to operate. But this is hardly damning evidence that religious giving amounts to throwing money down a rat hole, or that religious people's charity somehow "doesn't count." The religious person interested in the spiritual needs of a drug addict as well as his or her physical problems will see the effectiveness of a faith-based drug rehabilitation program (and the need for private charity for that program) differently from the secular person who is interested only in the nonfaith outcomes. A secularist views fostering the faith of a drug addict as a waste of resources, but the religious person sees it as essential to true rehabilitation. It would hardly be surprising that the faith-based approach to combating addiction costs more: Its goals are more ambitious.[21]

Secularists might make the excuse that they neglect to give because they are less subject to impure motives, such as fear or guilt. It's hard to deny that fear and guilt exist for some religious people. Within the Christian faith, for example, Jesus teaches his followers that to withhold charity from the needy is to withhold it from Christ himself: "Verily I say unto you, Inasmuch as ye did [it] not to one of the least of these, ye did [it] not to me." What will become of the nongivers? "And these shall go away into everlasting punishment: but the righteous into life eternal." Secularists often ask whether giving solely for the sake of avoiding "everlasting punishment" is charitable.[22]

Again, I argue that judging motives is misguided. Charity is a behavior, not a motive. Duty, guilt, and fear do not change the reality of a giver's gift; they only define what is in a giver's heart. And who are we to say what lies in the hearts of others—especially when they are giving? To condemn another's motives for behaving charitably is the very type of moral intrusion that secularists frequently despise in "religious fundamentalists."

~

The relationship between faith and charity is connected to American politics. Religious people are far more charitable than secularists; and religious people are disproportionately politically conservative. Conversely, relatively uncharitable secularists are especially likely to be politically liberal. One of the best explanations for the right-left charity gap is the link between faith and politics.

There is no denying the existence of this link. For example, in 1999, a self-identified conservative was almost twice as likely to attend his or her house of worship weekly than a self-described liberal; a liberal was nearly twice as likely as a conservative never to attend. The ideological differences go beyond attendance, however. Conservatives were 26 percent more likely than liberals to belong to a house of worship (whether or not they attended), 51 percent more likely to pray every day, and 30 percent more likely to say they devoted effort to their spiritual lives. Liberals were also generally less favorably disposed than conservatives toward believers and houses of worship. For example, liberals in 2002 were less sympathetic than conservatives to Catholics, the Catholic Church, Protestants, and, especially, fundamentalist Protestants.[23]

The political-religious divide, a source of significant bitterness in modern America, has played a major role in reshaping the modern Democratic and Republican parties. It is established wisdom on the political left that the so-called "religious right"—Christian evangelicals holding conservative political views—are in firm control of the Republican Party. This belief was never in greater evidence than in the 2004 election, when George W. Bush, an openly evangelical Christian, was elected president. After the election, liberal political Web sites posted a satirical election map depicting the Southern and Midwestern core of the United States that had gone for Mr. Bush as "Jesusland." Meanwhile, the states that went for John F. Kerry were blended with Canada and called the "United States of Canada."

American liberals have opposed what they characterize as a conservative theocracy. The liberal group Americans United for the Separation of Church and State is specific: "The single greatest threat to church-state separation in America is the movement known as the Religious Right. Organizations and leaders representing this religio-political crusade seek to impose a fundamentalist Christian viewpoint on all Americans through government action." The American mainstream media, largely uncritical of this assessment, regularly reports on the power and influence of Christian conservatives.[24]

But is it true that the religious right is an unparalleled force in American politics? Less remarked upon by the media is the political power of the secular left. Research using data on voting and voters' attitudes has demonstrated that liberal secularists are as influential in molding the platform of the American Democratic Party as are Christian conservatives for the Republicans.

The power of the secular left is particularly evident when we look at the Democratic "party faithful"—delegates to the Democratic National Convention who select the party's presidential nominee. For example, in 1972, more than a third of the white delegates to the 1972 convention that nominated George McGovern were secularists—atheists, agnostics, or simply people who seldom or never attended religious services. This was considerably higher than the secularist proportion of the U.S. population at the time, and it was a harbinger of things to come. By 1992, 60 percent of white delegates at the Democratic Convention (who nominated Bill Clinton) were secularists. Most surveys from the early 1990s estimated that no more than a quarter of the U.S. population could be classified as secularists, meaning that these hardcore Democrat activists were more than twice as likely as the population at large to reject traditional religious practice.[25]

Americans increasingly believe not only that the secular left controls the Democratic Party but that the party itself is hostile to religion. For example, the Pew Center for the People and the Press, which annually polls Americans on their views about religion and politics, found that 42 percent of Americans in 2003 believed the Democratic Party's attitude toward religion was friendly. This fell to 40 percent in 2004, and plummeted to 29 percent in 2005. In contrast, 55 percent felt that the Republican Party was friendly toward religion in 2005.[26]

The transformation of the Democratic Party into the party of secularism came about in a relatively short time. Consider how retrograde the words of President John F. Kennedy's 1961 inaugural address sound today: "With a good conscience our only sure reward, with history the final judge of our deeds, let us go forth to lead the land we love, asking His blessing and His help, but knowing that here on earth God's work must truly be our own." Or, as President Lyndon B. Johnson, also a Democrat, declared in introducing his voting-rights bill in 1965, "God will not favor everything that we do. It is rather our duty to divine His will." These would probably be career-ending remarks for a Democratic politician in 2006.[27]

If this book were not based on data, it would be tempting to tell a "two Americas" story in black-and-white terms—a story of one nation that is religious, conservative, and charitable, and another coexistent nation that is entirely secular, liberal, and uncharitable. The truth is that conservatives only *tend* to be more religious and charitable than liberals. There are still plenty of religious liberals, secular conservatives, and charitable (and selfish) people in both groups.

Still, religious liberals and secular conservatives go against the grain in contemporary American culture. So let's look at them and compare them with the more familiar religious conservatives and secular liberals. They give us some useful information about the charity we can expect to see if current political and religious trends continue. They lead to the prediction that the black-and-white "two Americas" story, though never completely accurate, will likely become more so in the future.

Religious Conservatives

Religious conservatives are the largest group of the four, at 19.1 percent of the American population in 2000—more than 50 million people. In most ways, they "look" like the population as a whole: They earn household incomes on a par with the national average, they are racially comparable to the country as a whole, and they possess average levels of education. Religious conservatives are substantially older than average and are far more likely than the rest of the population to be married.

Religious conservatives are the most prominent group in mainstream Christianity, making up 24 percent of all Protestants and 19 percent of Catholics. Among traditionalist Christian groups, however, they are dominant. For example, about half of Mormons are religious conservatives, as are about half of those who attend so-called "fundamentalist" denominations such as Full Gospel and Assemblies of God. They are underrepresented among less rigorous denominations such as the Episcopalians (12 percent), and almost completely absent from the most liberal churches, such as the Unitarians (2 percent). "In general, they are also rare among non-Christians, such as Jews, Buddhists, Moslems, and Hindus—although there are certainly groups of religious conservatives in these communities as well. For example, there are some reports that seven out of ten Orthodox Jews voted for George W. Bush in the 2004 presidential election."[28]

Of the four groups, religious conservatives are the most likely to give away money each year (91 percent), although this level is not much larger than that of religious liberals. They give away the most dollars per year ($2,367 versus $1,347 per household in the country as a whole). Religious conservatives volunteer at a rate that is 10 percentage points higher than the population average (67 percent per year). Contrary to popular belief, religious conservatives are more likely to give to secular charities than the overall population. In sum, religious conservatives are as charitable, or more so, than any other part of the population, including to secular causes.

Secular Conservatives

In contrast to religious conservatives, secular conservatives represent a small portion of the population, at 7.3 percent (about 20 million Americans). They look dramatically different than religious conservatives. Secular conservatives tend to be single men of low income and little education. On average, they earn 10 percent less per year than the population average. They are 48 percent more likely to drop out of high school than the population (and twice as likely as secular liberals), and 26 percent less likely to hold a college degree.

Like secular liberals, secular conservatives are not civically involved, and when it comes to giving and volunteering, secular conservatives are the least charitable group of the four (although secular liberals give them a run for their nondonated money). They are nearly 30 percentage points less likely to give to all charities each year than religious conservatives, and 16 points less likely to give to secular charities. They give only about a quarter as many dollars as religious conservatives ($661 per year, on average). They are 16 points less likely to volunteer, and do so less than half as often as religious conservatives (and only about a third as often as religious liberals). Secular conservatives behave less charitably than others in informal ways. For example, they are less likely than average to let someone in front of them in a line, to give up a seat on the bus, to give a stranger directions, and to help a homeless person.

Secular Liberals

Secular liberals are the second largest group, at 10.5 percent of the population (nearly 30 million Americans, in 2000). They are demographically distinct from religious conservatives: much younger (forty versus forty-nine, on average), more likely to be single (63 percent likely, versus 36 percent for religious conservatives), and have a considerably higher level of education (46 percent have college degrees or higher, compared with 33 percent of religious conservatives). It might come as a surprise to some that secular liberals also have the highest average income of the four groups, and are the most likely to be white.

Obviously, secular liberals are not affiliated with a house of worship. Although they do participate in some civic groups, their participation is meager. For example, they are less likely than religious conservatives to belong to college or professional fraternities (in spite of having higher rates of college attendance), and less likely to participate in sports, cultivate a hobby, or join a book club. However, they are more likely to belong to an association to which they only pay a fee (such as the Sierra Club or the National Organization for Women).[29]

Secular liberals are poor givers. They are 19 percentage points less likely to give each year than religious conservatives, and 9 points less likely than the population in general. They are even slightly less likely to give to specifically secular charities than religious conservatives. They give away less than a third as much money as religious conservatives, and about half as much as the population in general, despite having higher average incomes than either group. They are 12 points less likely to volunteer than religious conservatives, and they volunteer only about half as often. They are less generous than others in many informal ways as well. For example, they are significantly less likely than the population average to return excess change mistakenly given to them by a cashier.

Religious Liberals

Religious liberals make up the smallest of the four groups, comprising just 6.4 percent of the population (approximately 18 million Americans). Demographically, they most resemble the religious conservatives. Both groups are more or less the same age, and earn about the same amount of money. In two ways they are a demographically distinctive group, however. First, they are by far the most likely to belong to minority groups. For example, fully 23 percent of religious liberals are African American—a level about twice as high as any other of the four groups, or of the population in general. Second, they are 21 percent more likely than the population in general to hold a bachelor's degree or higher. Only secular liberals have a higher average level of education.

Black and white religious liberals have very little in common. Black religious liberals are scattered across various theologically conservative Christian denominations, such as the Baptists and the historically black African Methodist Episcopalians. In contrast, white religious liberals are disproportionately represented among theologically liberal denominations, such as the Unitarians and the Christian Scientists, as well as unusual religious groups, such as New Age religion and Paganism.

Religious liberals—especially African American religious liberals—participate actively in their communities. For example, they are more likely than people in the other groups to belong to political associations, fraternal organizations, neighborhood associations, and organizations dedicated to youths and schools.

Religious liberals bear a resemblance to religious conservatives in their giving habits. They are almost as likely to give (91 percent), but give away about 10 percent less money than religious conservatives each year. On both of these measures, they greatly exceed population averages. They are about as likely to give to secular causes as religious conservatives. Two-thirds volunteer each year. They are a bit less likely than religious conservatives to volunteer for religious causes, and a bit more likely to volunteer for nonreligious causes.

The bottom line for charity on the nexus of politics and religion is this: Religious people are far more charitable than secularists, no matter what their politics. But although religious conservatives are common, religious liberals are a fairly exotic breed. Liberals are far more likely to fall in the "secular" category than the "religious" category, and this is one big reason liberals as a group tend to look uncharitable.

What does the strong relationship between religious faith and conservatism augur for the future of American politics? We might logically expect the two groups most apparently out of sync with their political homes—religious liberals and secular conservatives—to dwindle in size as they find their religious beliefs (or lack thereof) are more in tune with people outside their political parties than within them. Some might change their political alignments—Republicans should suffer attrition of secular conservatives, and Democrats should lose some of their religious liberals. So far, this prediction about party shifting is only half right. Most recent studies show that the American population as a whole is shifting away from the Democratic Party and toward the GOP. But while religious Democrats are 30 percent more likely than the average among all Democrats to become Republicans, secular Republicans are *less* likely than the Republican average to become Democrats. Indeed, religious Democrats are three and a half times more likely to change party than are secular Republicans. As a result, the Democratic Party promises to become ever more the party of un-charity. The increasing secularization of the Democrats means downward pressure on charitable behavior among liberals.

Most Americans are charitable, just as they are religious, so the anticharity, secularist tilt of the American left can only be to the benefit of the American right wing, politically. The left, by rejecting mainstream American values such as charity and religious faith, will marginalize itself—a prediction made by many political commentators over the past two decades.

Should American conservatives be celebrating? I don't think so. On the contrary, anybody who believes—as I do—that charity is a key characteristic of a good and healthy society will join me in regretting the clear downward pressure on giving among the secularizing left. The division of America into religious givers and nonreligious nongivers should be cause for concern for all of us—left and right, secular and religious—and a call for ideas on how people of good will of all beliefs can be brought in greater numbers into the ranks of the charitable.

CHAPTER 3

OTHER PEOPLE'S MONEY

*A society that has more justice is a society
that needs less charity.*

RALPH NADER, 2000 GREEN PARTY
CANDIDATE FOR U.S. PRESIDENT[1]

Benjamin Franklin tells an interesting story in his autobiography
about the founding of a charity hospital in Philadelphia. A
friend of Franklin's was having trouble raising sufficient funds to
start the hospital, and he turned to Franklin—a prodigious
fund-raiser for other causes—for help. Franklin raised a good
deal of private money, but not enough to complete the project.
He decided to ask the Pennsylvania State Assembly for support.
To make the idea palatable to the members, he hatched an in-
genious scheme, which today we know as a "matching grant."
He wrote a funding bill in which the government would pay for
part of the hospital, but only if enough private charitable funds
were raised first. Franklin explained that Assembly members

could thus "take credit" for the private charity without spending any of their own money.[2]

As Franklin knew, politicians feel generous when they give away other people's money. This is as true today as it was in Franklin's time. For example, as one nears Albany, New York, on U.S. Interstate 90, it is impossible to miss the signs for "Joe Bruno Stadium." Built in 2002 with $14 million in funds taxed from New York State residents, this sports facility is named in honor of its *political* benefactor, the New York State Senate majority leader Joseph L. Bruno, the steward of the tax money used to build the stadium. But the most notorious purveyor of this sort of "generosity" is probably Senator Robert C. Byrd of West Virginia, who has dozens of government-funded buildings, monuments, and other projects named after him in his home state. These include the Robert C. Byrd Highway System, the Robert C. Byrd Bridge, the Robert C. Byrd Expressway, the Robert C. Byrd Federal Building, the Robert C. Byrd Health and Wellness Center, the Robert C. Byrd Institute for Advanced Flexible Manufacturing Systems, not to mention the numerous schools, factories, service centers, highway rest stops, and toll plazas throughout West Virginia.

Politicians are uniquely situated, one might think, when it comes to handing out favors at no expense to themselves. But we see the same behavior in vast swaths of "regular" people as well. A significant number of Americans (and Europeans as well) consider themselves charitable simply because they support policies of income redistribution through taxation. And this affects their private giving.

The relationship between charitable giving and ideas about income redistribution is by no means obvious. In fact, before I started the research for this book, I assumed that those people most concerned and vocal about economic inequality would be the *most* likely to give to charity. But I was wrong. Instead, I found a large amount of data all pointing in the same direction: For many people, the desire to donate other people's money displaces the act of giving one's own. People who favor government income redistribution are significantly less likely to behave charitably than those who do not. Even if the policies they support do not come into effect, they are still far less likely to donate to charity. For many Americans, political opinions are a substitute for personal checks; but people who value economic freedom, and thus bridle against forced income redistribution, are far more charitable.[3]

In this chapter, we will see that charity and conservative views on forced income redistribution go hand in hand. As such, through its economic policies and preferences, the political left is effectively conceding a tremendous amount of moral authority to the right wing when it comes to charity.

In 1996, a large sample of Americans was asked to respond to this statement: "The government has a responsibility to reduce income inequality." Forty-three percent of respondents disagreed with this statement; 33 percent agreed.[4]

When it came to charity, these two groups were radically different. Not only were those who disagreed significantly more likely to give money to charity than those who agreed, they also gave away, on average, four times as much money per year. This is not simply an artifact of religious giving. On the contrary, those who disagreed gave about three and a half times as much money per year to specifically nonreligious charities as those who agreed. They gave more to every type of cause and charity: health charities, education organizations, international aid groups, and human welfare agencies. Those who disagreed even gave more to traditionally liberal causes, such as the environment and the arts.[5]

Of people expressing the strongest feelings, those who "disagreed strongly" that the government should reduce inequality gave an average of twelve times more than those who "agreed strongly." People disagreeing strongly also gave nine times more to secular causes than those agreeing strongly.[6]

People in favor of government income redistribution give less to charity, even when survey questions are framed in such a way that they might elicit a response favorable to redistribution. For example, a 2001 poll asked respondents to agree or disagree with the statement that "the government has a basic responsibility to take care of people who can't take care of themselves." A large majority (75 percent) agreed with the statement. But the 25 percent who disagreed were more likely than the others to give money both to secular and religious causes.[7]

Can this difference be explained by income? In fact, people who favor government income redistribution tend to earn less money than those who oppose it. For example, people in 2004 who thought the government "should do more to equalize incomes" earned 13 percent less money than those who did not think government should do more. Perhaps people with less money favor redistribution because they would be net recipients rather than net payers.

This sounds plausible, but it is wrong. Let's see what happens when we control for income, education, religion, age, gender, marital status, race, and political views. If two people are identical in all these ways, but one feels the government should redistribute income more and the other disagrees, the second person will be 10 percentage points more likely to make a contribution to charity. He or she will give $263 more to charity each year, and will give $97 more to secular causes. In other words, people in favor of forced income redistribution are privately less charitable than those who oppose it, regardless of how much money they earn.[8]

This pattern holds for other forms of charity as well, such as volunteering. One survey shows that Americans who believe that the government has a responsibility to reduce income inequality are substantially less likely to volunteer their time than people who do not believe this. They are less likely to volunteer for secular and religious causes. Further belying the claim that welfare supporters are more compassionate than welfare opponents, people who stated in a 2002 poll that they thought the government was "spending too little money on welfare" were less likely than those saying the government is "spending too much money on welfare" to give directions to someone on the street, return extra change to a cashier, or even to give food or money to a homeless person.[9]

Proponents of income redistribution even give less blood than opponents. In 2002, people who agreed that the government should improve living standards for the poor represented 28 percent of the population, but donated just 20 percent of the blood. Meanwhile, people who disagreed that the government should improve living standards—believing that "people should take care of themselves" instead—were 25 percent of the population, but donated 31 percent of the blood. If the entire population gave blood at the same rate as opponents of social spending, the blood supply would increase by more than a quarter. But if everyone in the population gave at the same rate as government aid advocates, the supply would drop by about 30 percent.

Why does support for government income redistribution efforts suppress charity? The most straightforward answer comes when this support translates into policy—when governments tax away people's earnings and pay for services that might otherwise be supported privately.

Government spending on charitable causes leads people to give less to charity. And not just liberals—the evidence is that everyone gives less privately when the government gives more. The most likely reason for this is that people tend to see government aid and private charity as substitutes: If the government takes my money to help others, I will lower my private giving. Economists have a name for this phenomenon: the "public goods crowding out effect," and it is a potent theory for opponents of "big government" because it suggests that taxing and spending may have less net impact on citizens' welfare than imagined.

Numerous studies have demonstrated that a dollar in government spending on nonprofit activities displaces up to 50 cents in private giving. The highest level of crowding out occurs in assistance to the poor and other kinds of social welfare services, an indication that government social spending for the needy benefits recipients far less than its face value. Although less than a full-blown indictment of the usefulness of public money, it still indicates that the true effects of government assistance are weaker than government officials and state proponents think they are. For a charity that is reliant on both public funding and private giving (such as a private university that receives public-sector grants and private philanthropy), this means that nothing is "free" about government support—it not only lessens the effect of fund-raising efforts but also makes an organization more dependent on the government.[10]

The "crowding out effect" has had significant but little-known consequences in American history. In a recent study, economists found evidence that Franklin Delano Roosevelt's New Deal programs sharply reduced churches' charitable giving to the poor: The researchers noticed a 30 percent drop in church-based charity from 1933 through 1939, as federal spending to aid the needy went from zero to more than 4 percent of GDP. The researchers concluded that government funds were directly responsible for nearly all the drop in private church charity.[11]

Just as historical changes in government spending have stimulated changes in giving behavior, differences in state welfare policies across the United States help explain some of the regional differences in charitable giving. One study from 1985 found that increases in cash transfers from state governments to the poor led people in those states to contribute less to charity in general. This conclusion is consistent with current data on welfare spending and private giving at the state level. California gives the average recipient of Temporary Aid to Needy Families (TANF), the best-known type of "welfare" support in America, nearly five times more money each month than Mississippi gives its average recipient. At the same time, middle-class Californians give only about two-thirds as much of their income to charity as middle-class Mississippians. Does charity correlate directly with welfare expenditures? Or are these differences from state to state a result of, say, different rates of church attendance? To answer this question, I turned to state-level data from 1997 to 2002. I found that, if a state increases its TANF spending by 10 percent, it can expect a charitable giving decrease of about 3 percent among its citizens.[12]

To understand this finding, compare Tennessee and New Hampshire. The average household income in Tennessee is 35 percent lower than in New Hampshire, and average TANF levels are 61 percent lower. Still, the charitable giving per person is slightly higher (in dollars) in Tennessee than in New Hampshire ($420 versus $405), and the percent of income donated, on average, is more than twice as high (4.3 percent versus 1.8 percent). We can predict, therefore, that were Tennessee to raise its average TANF payment to New Hampshire's level, it would, in the process, crowd out about 42 percent of charitable giving. Is this price too high to pay for greater welfare support? Some will say yes, others no.[13]

The relationship between welfare and private giving is not only one way: Just as an increase in government social spending displaces private giving, decreases in state funding stimulate charity. Nonprofits take advantage of this effect by using cuts in government funding as a fund-raising tool. "Adversity is the mother of donation," quips one philanthropy expert, noting that charitable giving rose by a third in real terms over the 1980s, when President Ronald Reagan's budgets were cutting spending on social programs.[14]

An interesting case of crowding-out-in-reverse in 2005 caught the attention of the media, when Mayor Michael Bloomberg of New York City increased his personal charity to local nonprofits. Mayor Bloomberg, a self-made billionaire, privately donated about $140 million in 2004 to more than eight hundred nonprofits, many of which were affected by falling city government spending—spending decreases for which Bloomberg himself was largely responsible. In other words, Bloomberg "crowded in" his own donations.

Predictably, the donations stirred controversy. To some, Bloomberg's actions were doubly virtuous—not only did he exercise fiscal restraint for the good of New York but he lessened the pain through his own generosity. Others disagreed: In one news story, the *New York Times* suggested that Bloomberg was simply buying out his opposition: "All incumbents dispense favors. But Mr. Bloomberg's personal wealth has made him a modern-day Medici—a role that, some critics say, can also stifle dissent from institutions that have quietly absorbed city budget cuts because they worry that what the mayor gives he can also stop giving." From this cynical point of view, crowding out may be unfortunate, but Bloomberg's charity may be even worse because of the assumed strings attached to the private support supplanting government money.[15]

"Crowding out" only explains lower personal giving if the government is taxing citizens and redistributing the income to people and organizations in need. If increased government spending is only an idea or a political position, however, it should not affect giving behavior, correct? In other words, I might stop giving if the government picks up the support for my favorite charity, but not just because I think the government *should* do so, right?

No. The evidence at the beginning of this chapter connects charity with beliefs, not policies. The data tell us that it matters little whether the government is actually redistributing income and lessening inequality—what appears to displace charity is a person's *support* for these policies. People who think the government should redistribute income more are less likely to donate to charity than people who don't think so. This is nothing more than substituting political opinions for private donations. The opinions may or may not be sound, but the giving is conspicuously absent.

Politically, this is a left-right issue—because income redistribution is a left-right issue in America. Indeed, although 77 percent of self-proclaimed political liberals say the government should redistribute income more than at present, only 24 percent of conservatives say this. Substituting political belief for personal sacrifice shows a lack of tangible personal responsibility toward others in need and represents a deeply troubling relationship between ideology and personal action on the political left.[16]

Examples of this pattern are easy to find. Consider how various groups in America changed their charitable behavior between 2000 and 2002—from George W. Bush's contested first election victory to the year following the 9/11 terrorist attacks. The events of 9/11 stimulated a major spike in charitable giving and volunteering—the percentage of Americans who gave rose significantly from 2000 to 2002 in every poll.

One might expect the increase in private giving at this time to be especially high on the far left. In addition to 9/11, extreme liberals were suddenly facing an administration apparently less congenial to the ideals of income inequality than the Clinton administration had been, and which promoted tax policies that would lead to less total income redistribution than before. I expected to find people on the far left increasing their giving more than any other group in response to a president, who, they believed, intended to leave America's most vulnerable people out in the cold.

I was mistaken. From 2000 to 2002, the percentage of the American public who gave increased by 5 percentage points. But one group bucked the trend: the far left. In 2000, 70 percent of people who said they were "extremely liberal" gave money to charity each year. In 2002, the percentage giving among this group had *fallen* to 60 percent. In contrast, the percentage giving on the "extremely conservative" side rose from 84 to 95 percent.[17]

What's placing America's far left so far outside the charitable mainstream and exempting so many of them from a sense of personal charitable responsibility?

⸺

The American hard left has developed a resistance to charity. Consider the quotation that opens this chapter: "A society that has more justice is a society that needs less charity." For Ralph Nader, a vociferous champion of forced income redistribution, the existence of charity is evidence of an unjust society. We should make it obsolete—with government redistribution. In an ideal world there is no charity because there is no need for it.

This is an unrealistic worldview. We will never be free of need because our needs are constantly changing. In 1906, Americans' needs were different from those of 2006. Psychologists and economists have repeatedly shown that, above basic subsistence levels, the perception of "need" has mostly to do with what an individual sees others as having. Even if we could imagine a world without need, however, we would still want charity to be a part of it—because charity doesn't just affect the recipients. I will show later that charity is integral to the prosperity, health, and happiness of the givers themselves, as well as that of their communities and of our nation.[18]

Ralph Nader's is not the only liberal argument against charitable giving. John Steinbeck's famous rant against the evils of charitable giving not only typifies the thinking of some liberal intellectuals but excuses uncharitable behavior:

Perhaps the most overrated virtue in our list of shoddy virtues is that of giving. Giving builds up the ego of the giver, makes

him superior and higher and larger than the receiver. Nearly always, giving is a selfish pleasure, and in many cases is a down-
right destructive and evil thing. One has only to remember
some of the wolfish financiers who spent two thirds of their
lives clawing a fortune out of the guts of society and the latter
third pushing it back.[19]

The problem with charity, according to this creed, is that it reinforces the social hierarchy that comes from income inequality.
Givers are set up as good and virtuous, and "above" beneficiaries,
who are reduced to the role of grateful supplicants.

Indeed, it is true that charity reinforces a tangible class distinction between givers and receivers, especially when givers are
rich and recipients are poor. And although I am unaware of surveys that have asked this question, I am willing to bet that
many poor people prefer government aid—provided as a
right—to private charity, which requires gratitude and can be
withdrawn at the discretion of the giver. But would the poor
prefer no aid at all? If charity hurts one's self-esteem, does this
outweigh its benefits?

For some people on the political left who are deeply uncomfortable with social and economic class in America, the answer to
this question is yes. If there is any legitimate goal of philanthropy,
it is to promote *sharing* instead of providing aid. Authors expressing this point of view envision a world in which need is wiped
out: Everyone gives, everyone receives, and asymmetric gratitude
is nonexistent. Philanthropy is little more than a detail to enhance radical government income redistribution.[20]

History has not been kind to this worldview. Collectivist systems have been tried, most notably in Central and Eastern Europe, and they failed. The governments of the Communist bloc

ran inefficient systems that ultimately collapsed under their own bureaucratic weight. History has yet to vindicate the view that a society can prosper without private charity.

Many liberals believe that charitable giving has the unfortunate side effect of diminishing the self-esteem of the poor, and some even regret it because it strengthens class distinctions. But the most extreme leftist indictment of charity is that it is *intended* to harm the poor—it is a means for the rich to maintain strength. One professor and social critic expresses this viewpoint by charging that American charity has gone hand-in-glove with genocide and slavery:

> [T]he rhetoric of virtue has always coexisted with a deep-seated streak of violent repression in America: the physical and cultural genocide against American Indians, the enslavement of Africans, and the conquering of foreign lands. It is not merely that the rhetoric of caring and the roots of philanthropy are inadequate to assist those who need help, but that their very nature is tainted historically with visions of control over inferiors.[21]

It would be easy, but a mistake, to dismiss such hyperbole out of hand. In some circles, a strong philosophy abhors charity as just another tool of power. Usually, this philosophy stems from the core tenets of Marxism, which teaches: "From each according to his abilities, to each according to his needs."

Marxist philosophy has few open adherents in contemporary American political life, but it still thrives in the hothouses of academia, and is surprisingly common among artists, journalists, and intellectuals outside the United States. The basic Marxist argument about charity is that the rich give charitably because they can, but their actions are inherently corrupt because their control over the resources they enjoy is illegitimate. Not only is philanthropy no better than any other use of stolen property but it represents something worse: rank hypocrisy. The rich puff themselves up with the idea that they are doing something for the poor, but they only assuage their own guilt and mollify the masses, which might otherwise rise up against them. And they do all this with money they shouldn't have in the first place. The legendary American Socialist Party leader Eugene V. Debs employed this logic when he instructed his followers to refuse Andrew Carnegie's "blood money."[22]

These anticharity arguments rely on ideology as opposed to evidence, so I won't spend more time on them here. But I will raise one technical point: These positions depend on the assumption that givers are always rich, and recipients always poor. It is a common assumption, but it is wrong—as the next chapter will demonstrate.

"Social hierarchy" and Marxist philosophy might seem a little highfalutin' for most rank-and-file liberals, who probably never think in these terms. But make no mistake: Income inequality is a core *liberal* issue, and this is the link between redistribution and charity. This is not to say that no one on the right cares about economic inequality—that is not so—but it is the issue that most strongly separates liberals and conservatives today.

When Americans were asked in 2004 whether they thought income inequality in our society is too large, 76 percent of self-described liberals answered affirmatively, versus 41 percent of conservatives. Although 67 percent of liberals said they thought income inequality is a "serious problem," only 25 percent of conservatives agreed with them. When it comes to concern about income inequality and support for government attempts to mitigate it, one's politics matter more even than one's income. In 2004, upper-income liberals were 22 percentage points more likely than lower-income people of all political persuasions to say that income inequality was too large. This means that low-income Americans are less disturbed by income inequality than are rich liberals.[23]

These differences on whether income inequality is a problem lead to differences in what to *do* about it—forcibly redistribute income or not—which, as we know, represents a wedge between liberal and conservative giving. Those who see inequality as a major problem in America usually want to solve it through government action. Among the Americans in 2004 who said they thought income inequality in the United States was a "serious problem," 71 percent also thought the government should redistribute income more to solve the problem. Meanwhile, among people who didn't think inequality was a serious problem, only 41 percent advocated more government action. Similarly, 64 percent of people saying the United States is becoming a society of "haves and have-nots" thought that government should do more, versus only 25 percent who did not characterize American society in this way.[24]

Why do average liberals worry so much about income inequality? Many feel it is simply unfair and unjust that some Americans struggle to make their rent each month while others live in luxury. Congressman Bernie Sanders (the only socialist in the U.S. Congress) sums up the view of many: "There is something fundamentally wrong and very dangerous about a society in which so few have so much and so many have so little." Many liberals also believe that economic inequality is the source of other social problems. If some people are very rich and others very poor, there arise public health and welfare implications. This is a real issue in many parts of the developing world—where super-rich aristocracies coexist with populations living in starvation and misery—and many believe it is a problem in America, too.[25]

Opposition to charity has not always been associated with leftism in America. In the late nineteenth and early twentieth centuries, such a position was more often associated with the political right; but this is hardly surprising since conservative ideology in America traditionally stood opposed to *dependence* on any sort of handout. Dependency, many conservatives traditionally believed, degrades the poor, discourages work, and raises crime rates. Thus Andrew Carnegie's lament: "It were better for mankind that the millions of the rich were thrown in to the sea than so spent as to encourage the slothful, the drunken, the unworthy."

A century ago, some went even further, however. According to one extreme line of reasoning—blessedly rare today—dependent people are flawed by their very nature. By giving aid and comfort to the underperformers in society, charity promotes the worst in society by artificially helping the weak to survive and bring forth new generations of underperformers.[26]

The intellectual roots of this kind of thinking can be traced to the nineteenth-century British philosopher Herbert Spencer, the father of so-called "Social Darwinism," and coiner of the term "survival of the fittest." Adherents of Social Darwinism believed that observed inequalities between people represented a natural process by which the "fit" (successful people) rose to the top of social and economic hierarchies, and the "unfit" (the poor and needy) were weeded out. Since political and social institutions (such as welfare and charity) cannot permanently alter this process, the thinking went, these institutions created a disservice to society by delaying the inevitable population decline of the unfit. These institutions created pain by providing artificial incentives for the unfit to reproduce.[27]

This sort of philosophy may sound radically right wing to modern ears, reminiscent of Ayn Rand (who said that "suffering is not a claim check, and its relief is not the goal of existence") and her like. But it was not limited to the right; Social Darwinism also found a home among certain groups of utopian leftists. Margaret Sanger, the pioneer for birth control who founded Planned Parenthood was a Social Darwinist, and she promoted contraceptives to discourage the reproduction of "unfit" people. In her 1920 book *Woman and the New Race,* Sanger defined birth control as "nothing more or less than the facilitation of the process of weeding out the unfit, of preventing the birth of defectives or of those who will become defectives."[28]

Today, it is difficult to find anyone—liberal or conservative—who would publicly state that we should let the needy perish and so improve society. The closest we come is the view in some ultra-capitalist circles that charity, because it employs nonmarket forces, is a bad way to care for the poor. One author on the subject writes, "I expect little good to come from charity. I prefer unfettered, unrestrained capitalism, which I consider to be the absolute best 'welfare state' there is." Why? "Whereas business is an inherently efficient activity, charity is inherently wasteful." It goes without saying that this viewpoint is as aberrant to most people's sensibilities as is the assertion that charity is a tool with which to harm the poor. Not only is it morally bankrupt, it is false. As any economics student can tell you, there are all sorts of activities in which for-profit businesses are less efficient than nonprofits. There are many important services (such as the operation of houses of worship) for which no viable for-profit business models exist.[29]

As we can see, the relationship between charity and political ideology has shifted over time. And this means that liberals aren't necessarily locked into a worldview that opposes charity, any more than conservatives are locked into a worldview that supports it. At this moment in history, American conservatism is informed by core values—support for religion and opposition to the welfare state—that strongly support charitable behavior. Inasmuch as the Democratic Party is the party of economic redistribution and of secularism, it actively discourages charitable behavior. This could change, and I hope it will, because charity should transcend party. Whether is does or not depends on the honesty and leadership of charitable liberals.[30]

The evidence in this chapter provides yet another explanation for the paradox laid out at the beginning of the book: How is it that liberals, who often claim to care more about others than conservatives do, are personally less charitable? The answer is most likely not that average liberals are purposely disingenuous—it is that they often confuse political ideology with actual giving. Liberals' views on income inequality and forced income redistribution cloud their ability to behave in charitable ways. Conservatives are far more sanguine about the ill effects of income inequality, and unsympathetic to forced income redistribution because it interferes with economic freedom and private opportunity. This leaves them in a better frame of mind for private charity.

For many everyday liberals, income inequality is a societal problem—one that may be accentuated and legitimized by private giving and ameliorated by government income redistribution. Conservatives do not share the view that income inequality is a systemic problem. Rather, they view it as a phenomenon that affects individuals—at worst, an unfortunate reflection of some people's bad luck or poor choices in life; at best, an important stimulus for people to strive for more in a dynamic market economy such as America's. This is a critical difference between today's political left and right.

This difference helps explain a crucial and much-debated fact about contemporary American politics: Although the poor may benefit directly from redistributive policies, they have increasingly turned against the Democratic Party, which supports them. For example, in the 2004 presidential election, Mr. Bush won all ten of the poorest American states in 2003 (measured in per capita personal income), as well as twenty-one of the bottom twenty-five—many by wide margins. These results surprised many liberal commentators—as Thomas Frank asked in the title of his best-selling book, *What's the Matter with Kansas?* Frank went on to explain that conservatives have cleverly appealed to the poor in rural, low-income areas by focusing on "cultural" issues such as abortion and gun rights. As a consequence, poor voters have been distracted from the *real* issues, such as socioeconomic inequality. In other words, the poor simply do not know what's good for them.[31]

Frank viewed the evidence through the liberal lens, but he reached the wrong conclusion. His explanation is redolent of Marx's notion that the poor are subject to a "false consciousness." No doubt this idea is reassuring to liberals: It provides a convenient explanation for the rightward shift in voting patterns over the past decades—an explanation that in no way challenges liberals to think about the weaknesses of their own positions.

The most obvious reason why working Americans increasingly tend to vote for conservative politicians is that they think these politicians are *morally right* in refusing to expropriate more resources from America's wealthy. This view can be defended as fairness just as strenuously as income redistribution can. The argument goes like this: Some people work hard and earn a lot of money; it is unfair to take it away just because they have more than others.

This reasoning might discount too much the role that forces such as luck and discrimination play in success in modern America. But to focus only on these forces is to ignore the importance of opportunity and freedom as animating values to all classes of Americans, including the working poor.

One famous anecdote illustrates the political cost of denying this fact. In 1972, George McGovern, the Democratic presidential candidate, gave a campaign speech to workers at a rubber factory near Akron, Ohio. He announced his plan to raise inheritance taxes significantly and so level the playing field—that is, minimize the economic privileges that are handed down from generation to generation in America. To McGovern's shock, the audience booed him—even though the policy would have benefited them, as lower middle-class workers, directly in the form of redistributed taxes, and indirectly in the form of diminished socioeconomic stratification.

The general unpopularity of the "death tax" is still utterly befuddling to many liberals who favor posthumous income leveling. Once again, there is a simple explanation: People of all income classes believe that everyone should have the freedom to be as generous as they want with their own money.[32]

And this brings us back to giving, whether to strangers or to one's own children. If there is a false consciousness at work in the debate about income redistribution in America, it is not the poor's refusal to rise up and demand that others hand over more of their incomes. Rather, it is the liberal confusion between political opinions and charity.

Reasonable people will always probably disagree over whether incomes in America are too unequal, and thus whether governments should redistribute resources between the rich and the poor more or less than at present. One thing we do know is that one side of this debate faces downward pressure on its private charity—even, it turns out, when its support for income redistribution is nothing more than a political opinion with no reflection in public policies. Although redistribution might be desirable, and one's political support for it merited, this support is *not* the same thing as voluntary giving. Furthermore, if support for a policy that does not exist (such as large-scale income redistribution in the United States) substitutes for private charity, the needy are left worse off than before. It is one of the bitterest ironies of liberal politics today that political opinions are apparently taking the place of help for others.

CHAPTER 4

INCOME, WELFARE,
AND CHARITY

Not he who has much is rich, but he who gives much.
ERICH FROMM[1]

Matel Dawson, Jr., was born in Shreveport, Louisiana, in 1921. The fifth of seven children in a poor family, Dawson dropped out of school after eighth grade to go to work. Shreveport presented limited opportunities, so when he was nineteen he went to work for the Ford Motor Company in Detroit. Dawson worked for Ford for more than sixty years, retiring at eighty-one as a forklift operator. From the beginning, his life at Ford was a common kind of American success story: He worked long hours, skipped vacations, and invested in Ford's employee stock plan; by the end of his career, he earned $100,000 a year. Charmingly, he attributed his prosperity to "the grace of Almighty God and the Ford Motor Company."[2]

The unexpected part of Mr. Dawson's story is this: He gave nearly all his money away. During his life, he contributed $1.3 million to charity. This included $680,000 in gifts to Wayne State University in Detroit, $300,000 to Louisiana State University, and $240,000 to the United Negro College Fund. He also contributed thousands to his church, other schools, and civil rights organizations. Dubbed the "forklift philanthropist" by the press, Matel Dawson became a celebrity of sorts, appearing on national television and receiving an invitation to the White House to meet President Bill Clinton. Journalists were astonished by this working man's willingness to be so philanthropic. When they asked why he gave so much, he gave simple, straightforward responses. "I just want to help people, leave a legacy, and be remembered," he said.

Matel Dawson's charity runs counter to the way many people think giving is supposed to work: People who give a lot have to be rich. All too often, when I tell people about my research, I get the response: "Of course people in favor of government income redistribution don't give to charity—they're most likely to be poor, so they can't afford to give." This theory cuts across political views. In a 1986 television interview, Margaret Thatcher, the former British prime minister, quipped, "No one would remember the Good Samaritan if he'd only had good intentions—he had money, too." A good line, to be sure, but is the assumption behind it sound?

Perhaps not. After all, we have seen that religious people tend to give much more time and money than secular people, whether they are poor or rich. And rich people who favor forced income redistribution give less frequently than poor people who do not favor income leveling. Furthermore, many kinds of charity, such as volunteering or behaving compassionately toward others, are nonfinancial, so income has little economic reason to affect them.

It's time to nail down the true relationship between income and giving. This relationship holds some surprises, and it tells us more about American charity and selfishness.

People with lots of money give most of the *dollars* to charity in the United States, an obvious point about income and charity. The top 10 percent of households in income are responsible for at least a quarter of all the money contributed to charity, including a fifth of the money contributed to religious organizations—mostly churches—and about a third of the money to secular causes. Households with total wealth exceeding $1 million (about 7 percent of the American population) give about half of all charitable donations. Simply put, your local United Way would close down were it not for rich people in your community.[3]

Just as people purchase more of most goods and services as their incomes increase, so, too, they give more money away to charity. But *how much* more do they give when their incomes rise? The answer has significant implications for the health of charities themselves as average prosperity climbs nationwide; it could also help predict the effects of a recession on charitable giving.

The most common way to measure the relationship between changes in charity and income is by looking at the percentage increase in giving associated with a 10 percent increase in income. Most research has found this to be in the neighborhood of 7 percent, even after controlling for other forces, such as education, age, and race. For example, imagine a family that earns $50,000 per year and gives $1,000 to charity. If they receive an income increase of 10 percent, to $55,000, the data suggest that they will most likely increase their giving to about $1,070. An income decrease down to $45,000 would mean a giving drop to about $930. This is a good news-bad news story for charitable organizations. On the one hand, it means that donations tend to grow more slowly (if measured in percentages) than the whole economy; on the other, it means that during a recession charities tend to be hurt less than the economy as a whole.[4]

The impact on charity from changes in wealth (the value of people's savings, investments, and property), as opposed to income, is somewhat less dramatic. Economists estimate that a 10 percent increase in the amount of wealth people have increases their giving by about 3 percent. It makes sense that because people protect their savings to ensure an income source in the future, for themselves or their heirs, this effect would be more muted than that from income. Still, the wealth effect on giving can be significant, and even the key to a giving boom, as it was in the late 1990s. From 1995 through 2000, inflation-adjusted income per capita increased by 12 percent; but when the stock market boom and increases in house values boosted average household wealth, household giving exploded by 54 percent. Obviously, these types of wealth tend to be unpredictable, compared with regular savings, which is currently 0 percent of America's national income—the lowest level since the Great Depression. This is cause for worry: When wealth is growing because of stocks, bonds, and real estate markets, giving becomes volatile and so exposes charities, churches, and other causes to risk.[5]

Although it makes sense that people with higher incomes and wealth would give away more *dollars* than people with lower incomes, it is not apparent that they would necessarily be more *likely* to make a contribution (of any size), but this also is true. Poor American families are less likely than middle-class families to give to charity, and the middle class is less likely to contribute than the rich. About nine families in ten in the top income quintile (the top 20 percent of earners) give charitably each year, as compared with about six in ten families in the bottom quintile. People often explain that the rich are so likely to give because of a so-called "culture of elite philanthropy"—the idea that wealthy people not only experience social pressure to give generously but derive prestige from their giving as well. One scholar who interviewed the wealthiest givers in New York in the 1990s found that this culture also features a significant element of secular duty—wealthy people report feeling an obligation to give generously because they have been blessed financially.[6]

The effects of income on nonmoney giving, such as volunteering, are not so obvious. On the one hand, although people's wages vary widely, we all have an equal endowment of time: twenty-four hours every day, whether we're rich or poor; on the other hand, as people make more money, the value of their volunteer time becomes higher. This is what economists call "opportunity cost." For example, the opportunity cost of an hour of a lawyer's time is higher than mine, because the hour's work foregone by the lawyer would have paid him or her much more than I can make as a university professor. One would therefore assume that, all else being equal, the lawyer will volunteer less than I will. Despite the theoretical possibility that the rich might volunteer less than the poor because of the opportunity cost of time, research has found little connection between income and volunteering. Time gifts are freer of economic class than money gifts.[7]

The relationship between income and charity is even more complicated for informal giving. High-income people are more likely than the poor to give in some informal ways, but not in others. For example, rich people are much more likely than poor people to give money to neighbors, friends, and strangers. People with high incomes are also more likely to give blood, and they give directions to strangers on the street more frequently than people with low incomes. However, the poor are more likely to give a homeless person food or money. In other words, if you find yourself in a strange city and need directions, ask a rich person. If you need a sandwich, ask a poor person.

The special compassion of the poor toward the homeless is unsurprising because people tend to contribute to causes that have affected them personally, or might affect them some day. In one 2000 survey in which people were asked their reasons for charitable giving, 59 percent of respondents—74 percent of the people who gave—said that one of their main giving motives was that the charities they supported had once helped them or someone they knew.[8]

The total dollars given and the likelihood of giving are not necessarily the best ways to measure money charity, however. In earlier chapters, we looked at money giving as a percentage of family income, because it is one way to gauge the relative "sacrifice" a family makes. For example, a family earning $100,000 and giving $2,000 obviously contributes more money than a family earning $25,000 but giving $1,000. But the sacrifice made by the poorer family (4 percent) is double that of the first. Measuring charity this way makes the poor look much better than doing so with the dollars given or the likelihood of giving. Indeed, all the available data tell us that poor people contribute more of their household incomes than rich people do. Most studies have shown that the poor tend to give away between 4 and 5 percent of their incomes, on average, and the rich give away between 3 and 4 percent. Both groups give away significantly more than the middle class.[9]

That the poor give the most is especially impressive considering that the rich, middle class, and poor all face the same prices for necessities such as food and basic housing (although one can pay more than the bare minimum for these things)—so a certain percentage sacrifice in giving by the poor is more meaningful than the same percentage for the rich. For example, imagine a family earning $20,000 that gives 5 percent to charity. This family has $19,000 left over for its basic needs. The family earning $100,000 and making the same percentage gift has $95,000 left over.

A few common explanations, which usually focus on the cultural forces for giving, such as religion, tell why the poor sacrifice the most. For example, the religious congregations that low-income people belong to tend to be especially demanding about tithing. In 2000, poor American families were roughly twice as likely as middle-class families to be Seventh-Day Adventists, Pentecostals, or Jehovah's Witnesses. They were also significantly less likely to belong to more "mainline" (and less stringent) denominations such as the Episcopalians, Methodists, and Presbyterians.[10]

So what are we to take from all this? On the one hand, the poor are less charitable than others in the sheer likelihood of giving; on the other, they are *more* charitable when it comes to the average percentage of their incomes given away. So which is it? Are the poor more or less charitable than the rest of America?

The answer is both: The poor—like the rest of America—are divided starkly into givers and nongivers. Some impoverished Americans are the most charitable members of our society, but others give virtually nothing at all. Families that gave a positive amount to charity but that earned less than $20,000 in 2000, for example, donated more than 7 percent of their family income—more than twice the percentage given by the givers earning more than $100,000 per year. But the poor also have an inordinately high number of nongivers—they are more than four times more likely not to give at all than people in the top income groups. A huge difference exists between poor givers and poor nongivers. When it comes to charity, we cannot simply refer to "the poor."

Where income comes from helps determine whether a poor family will give or not give. In the past, most economists studying the relationship between income and charity have made a crucial error: They have assumed that all kinds of income function in the same way. In other words, if I earn $100, I will do the same things with it—spend it, save it, or give it away—as if the government sends me a check for $100. This assumption is wrong. People are more likely to give away earned income, such as wages, than they are to give away unearned income, such as welfare from the government. Consider the data from 2003. Among a group of 7,000 American families, a little under 5 percent received some amount of "welfare" support, such as Temporary Aid to Needy Families (TANF, for poor families) or Supplemental Security Income (SSI, which provides support for the disabled). This does not include social security payments to the elderly, unemployment insurance, or any other "entitlement" payments to the nonpoor. People not receiving welfare gave about six times more money to charity, on average, than welfare recipients. They were also more than twice as likely to give any amount, and almost twice as likely to volunteer.[11]

To make a fair comparison, however, we need to hold income constant and compare the working poor with the nonworking poor—welfare versus low-income working families. For example, consider two families: One gets its income from earned wages; the other relies on government welfare support. Both families are close to the bottom of the income distribution, bringing in less than $14,000 annually. It is as likely as not that these households include children; for those that do, the average number is two. Statistics show that the nonwelfare family is most likely to live in a rural area, the welfare family in an inner city. These two families are likely to behave completely differently when it comes to charity. On average, the working poor family gives more than three times as much money to charity as the welfare family. It is more than twice as likely to give, and also almost twice as likely to volunteer. The working poor family is more likely to give to every type of charity than the welfare family, including religion, charities serving the poor, youth-related causes, international aid, and the environment.[12]

How much does welfare income depress giving? One study of American families in 1999 found that a dollar in welfare income for a family erased an average of 57 cents from its private charitable giving. A 10 percent increase in its average welfare payment lowered its charitable giving by about 1.4 percent. Similarly, an investigation of families in 2001 revealed that families not on welfare were about three times more likely to give and volunteer than families receiving welfare. Holding constant differences in education, age, race, and religion, the study also found that, although an increase in earned income drove giving and volunteering up, an increase in welfare drove giving and volunteering down.[13]

The most responsible reading of all this evidence is that it is not poverty per se that makes people uncharitable—but rather the government's conventional policies for eradicating it.

Why does welfare reduce charity? We know it is *not* because of poverty—because people with equivalent income from other sources give and volunteer generously—but there are several other possible explanations.

Critics of the American welfare system argue that welfare support reduces the self-sufficiency of the recipients, which in turn affects giving to charity. Welfare recipients also tend to be separated from healthy communities, and thus have few appealing opportunities to act charitably, few generous role models, and few expectations to give.

To understand these arguments, we must first understand how welfare works. Government welfare is basically an "entitlement" in most developed countries: If you live in the right type of household and meet certain requirements, you have a right to the support. Before World War II, the common conditions for receiving welfare support in the United States were poverty, and having at least one dependent child at home. There was also an explicit expectation of "acceptable" behavior; for example, bearing children outside marriage violated the conditions for welfare coverage in most states.

The American welfare system expanded enormously in the 1960s, under the aegis of President Lyndon B. Johnson's Great Society and War on Poverty initiatives. The resulting legislation expanded most welfare coverage and created many new programs—some of which still exist today, such as Medicare (free health insurance for senior citizens). During this period, the U.S. government dropped the condition that parents could qualify for support only if they were married. Indeed, from the 1960s until the mid-1990s (when the system was reformed), households could not qualify for the most prominent welfare program, Aid to Families with Dependent Children (AFDC), unless one of the child's parents—nearly always the father—was physically absent from the home.

Welfare support became many households' financial status quo, and it created a lot of dependence on the system. Many experts on the American welfare system have argued that unemployed people received support, lost job skills (or never acquired them), and became unable to gain stable employment, making them chronically reliant on state aid. During the early 1990s, welfare support in America extended beyond a year for about half of recipients, beyond two years for 30 percent, and beyond four years for more than 15 percent. Furthermore, nearly half of all the people who left welfare were back on the rolls within a year. Millions of people found themselves permanently on the dole.[14]

Most people would agree that this situation is far from ideal. Economic dependence is widely considered to be unnatural and degrading, so it seems sensible to predict that this reliance would depress all sorts of virtues, such as honesty, thrift, hard work— and probably charity as well. Centuries before the advent of the modern American welfare system, Thomas Jefferson uttered these words: "Dependence begets subservience and venality, suffocates the germ of virtue, and prepares fit tools for the designs of ambition." This is not a "conservative" idea; progressive leaders have notably said the same thing. President Franklin D. Roosevelt, in his 1935 State of the Union address, declared, "Continued dependence on [government support] induces a spiritual and moral disintegration fundamentally destructive to the national fiber. To dole out relief in this way is to administer a narcotic, a subtle destroyer of the human spirit." Even President Jimmy Carter, whose social policies expanded the American welfare system, called the system "anti-work" and "anti-family."[15]

Some observers have argued that the problem with unlimited welfare extends beyond chronic dependence among a set population. They contend that the system creates incentives for people to join; unless there are policy reforms, dependency grows over time. This means that welfare causes the very condition it seeks to relieve: People receive welfare because they are out of work, and some people choose not to work because of the existence of welfare. Communities thus spiral downward in a feedback loop of idleness and government aid. It is hard to test whether this is true, although whether or not it is, most people *think* so: More than 75 percent of Americans (and nearly 70 percent of the poor themselves) agree with this statement: "Welfare makes people work less than they would without a welfare system."[16]

Many middle-class Americans cannot comprehend how welfare could create incentives to join and become dependent; after all, it's a lifestyle featuring the twin degradations of long-term unemployment and subsistence-level support. Others wonder why some impoverished communities have high welfare dependence but others do not. To answer these questions, some experts study the peculiar culture of welfare recipients. One welfare scholar, the political scientist Lawrence Mead, believes that people from community-rich sociocultural backgrounds—such as Jewish and Asian immigrants—have traditionally relied on hard work and strong family and community ties to lift themselves out of poverty. Consequently, they are unlikely to fall into welfare dependence. In contrast, Mead believes that other poor groups have few community bonds to reinforce a work ethic and moral standards, and thus have slipped into chronic reliance on the government. According to Mead's argument, the government is complicit in this sorry situation because these dependent groups successfully petition for continued support rather than cultivate opportunities for education and work. If this view is correct, the connection between welfare and charity is obvious: A weak community gives a person little economic and moral support and hence few chances to advance. It provides few compelling reasons to behave charitably. And the government becomes the willing enabler.[17]

The noted sociologist William Julius Wilson makes an argument that bears some similarity to Mead's, although it places less emphasis on the character of welfare recipients and more on their living circumstances—even their physical surroundings. Wilson notes, for instance, that urban poor blacks in America are clustered into neighborhoods far-removed from those of middle-class people and mainstream market places. Casual observation of large public housing projects in major cities—in neighborhoods most people would not care to enter—bear out Wilson's point. This isolation of dependent populations means that the urban poor have fewer healthy economic role models. It is physically difficult to escape such neighborhoods—without cheap and easy transportation, people can't commute to jobs. Common sense tells us that people stuck in communities characterized by drugs, crime, unemployment, and government coverage of income and housing are unlikely to see a blossoming spirit of philanthropy.[18]

But perhaps there are different reasons for the lack of measurable giving and volunteering among welfare recipients. For instance, some researchers have suggested that giving among welfare recipients tends to be more informal than among other groups. For example, single mothers on welfare might baby-sit for each other. If the nonworking poor give disproportionately in ways they are unlikely to report on a survey, their measured levels of charitable giving might appear lower than others.[19]

This is a plausible argument and it appears strengthened because the poor give a higher proportion of their incomes to friends, neighbors, and strangers than the rich do. But once again, this informal charity occurs largely among the *working* poor. In 1999, people on welfare were less than half as likely as people not on welfare to give informally to friends or strangers.[20]

All the findings on welfare suggest that policy reforms that lower dependency should raise charity. And we have witnessed a behavioral transformation during the last decade because of changes to the welfare system, changes that raise optimism about giving by the nonworking poor.

By the mid-1990s, the welfare system was in tatters: expensive, unwieldy, dependency-creating, and wildly unpopular with the American public. Furthermore, from a charity perspective, the American welfare system before the mid-1990s was a disaster (although one did not hear this argument at the time). Fortunately, the system changed for the better in 1996, after Congress passed a series of reforms imposing time limits on how long people could receive welfare support and requiring that people work to receive benefits. These reforms were, and still are, good news for charity by the poor.[21]

Many people feared the worst from reforms that would limit the length of support, and they predicted great hardship among the poor as a result. One prominent children's advocate called the law an "outrage . . . that will hurt and impoverish millions of American children." Further, she predicted that it would "leave a moral blot on . . . our nation that will never be forgotten." The Urban Institute, a nonpartisan think tank in Washington, D.C., predicted that the law would push 2.6 million people (including 1.1 million children) into poverty.[22]

These doomsday scenarios never came to pass—quite the opposite. In the first seven years after the enactment of welfare reform in 1996, the poverty rate fell from 13.7 percent of the U.S. population to 12.5 percent—and this period covered an economic recession. Furthermore, according to the U.S. government, welfare reform helped to move 4.7 million Americans from welfare dependency to self-sufficiency within three years of enactment, and the welfare caseload declined by 54 percent from 1996 to 2004.[23]

Welfare reform might have had an impact on charitable giving because people become more charitable when they get off government support. For example, 20 percent of families on welfare in 2001 and 2003 gave to charity in 2003, and 9 percent volunteered. Among those on welfare in 2001 but *not* in 2003, however, 29 percent gave in 2003, and 16 percent volunteered. (Among families not on welfare in either period, 64 percent gave and 23 percent volunteered.)[24]

But is leaving welfare the reason these people gave and volunteered more? Perhaps the people most likely to give time and money to charity are the people most likely to get off welfare in the first place. In other words, there might be a force out there that makes needy people both charitable and resistant to long-term welfare dependency. A good candidate for such a force is religion: We already know that it makes people more generous than they otherwise would be. It might make them more self-reliant as well. The data from 2001 and 2003 provide some evidence of this. Families on welfare in 2001 and 2003 were more likely than families not on welfare in those years to say they had no religious affiliation. People on welfare in 2001 but off welfare in 2003 were less likely to be secularists than those on welfare both years, but more likely than those not on welfare in either year.[25]

This evidence would come as no surprise to many religious social service organizations. For generations, these organizations have applied religious faith in the rehabilitation of criminals and drug abusers, and those exhibiting other pathologies. One typical organization that uses Christian faith in providing job and life skills to prison inmates describes its programs as "anchored in biblical teaching that stresses personal responsibility, the value of education and work, care of persons and property and the reality of a new life in Christ." Just as faith helps former criminals become productive citizens, it might help resolve the problems leading some people to need welfare in the first place.[26]

George W. Bush's administration is banking on this idea. The White House's Office of Community and Faith-Based Initiatives promotes and supports the use of religious nonprofit organizations in delivering government-funded social services. This appears to be popular among conservatives and moderates, who are disproportionately religious. However, the political left objects that these initiatives represent an improper mingling of church and state.[27]

But perhaps the more important reason that liberals and conservatives diverge on faith-based initiatives in welfare reform is because, as was true in attitudes about government income redistribution, they have different ideas about the responsibilities of individuals. Many traditional liberals reject on ideological grounds the notion that problems such as poverty have their roots in the private behavior of the disadvantaged. According to many critics of the conservative faith-based movement, a person is not poor and on welfare because of her own poor choices and irresponsible behavior. Rather, her poverty comes from the society that has dealt her a bad hand—a society that consequently owes her support instead of trying to alter her character. Instead of using religious faith to help people pull themselves up, many on the left advocate an expansion of the welfare state itself to deliver to them the favorable circumstances they deserve as *rights*. To conservatives, the liberal point of view sounds a bit like prescribing liquor to treat an alcoholic: People need personal improvement and opportunities to help themselves, not more of the same treatment that created their dependency in the first place.[28]

Millions of pages have been written on the subject of the causes of poverty, and social scientists have yet to extract any definitive explanations. I certainly don't intend to here. I will simply point out that the relationship between welfare and charity raises important questions that have broader implications for how we alleviate poverty. Those who view poverty as a systemic problem will tend to advocate a secular, government-focused solution; those who see it as a problem of individual behavior will tend to favor private, religious, individual opportunity oriented solutions. This is not the place to adjudicate between these worldviews. I can, however, say with some certainty that the liberal solution will, at the very least, have the secondary consequence of lower charity; the private, faith-based solution will have a positive impact on giving. And higher charity will, as we shall see in a later chapter, radiate back into greater prosperity and a higher quality of life for the poor.

⌒

A further explanation for why political conservatives in America score higher on measures of giving than political liberals is that

the unusually charitable working poor are disproportionately politically conservative, but the relatively uncharitable nonworking
poor are much more liberal.

The few surveys that have probed both welfare receipt and
political beliefs in the same population have produced fairly clear
results. In 1986, for example, a person in the bottom income
quintile saying he or she had not received "income from AFDC,
General Assistance, SSI, or Food Stamps" was 34 percent more
likely to self-identify as a political conservative than someone
who received one of these types of welfare during the year. If two
people were identical with respect to religion, total income, education, gender, marital status, and race, but one collected welfare
and the other did not, the welfare recipient would be significantly
less likely to call himself or herself a conservative than the person
not on welfare.[29]

There are two possible explanations for this pattern. First,
low-income conservatives may be relatively unlikely to request
welfare assistance even when they are eligible to receive it. Inasmuch as conservative values include self-reliance and personal entrepreneurship, it stands to reason that a poor conservative would
be less likely than a poor liberal to request welfare assistance.

The other possibility is that welfare itself *makes* people more
liberal. Imagine a conservative person in need, entitled to welfare.
If she collects a check from the government, she might experience what psychologists call "cognitive dissonance," in which two
of her attitudes are inconsistent—dissonant—with each other.
On the one hand, as a conservative, she probably believes people
should support themselves and be self-reliant; on the other hand,
receiving money or services from the government is helpful to
her (at least in the immediate term). Humans, psychologists argue, find this kind of dissonance uncomfortable, and they seek to

resolve it by changing one of the attitudes. One way to do this is for her to decide that self-reliance is overrated and opportunity is an illusion, and become a liberal. I once heard it said that a quick way to make a liberal into a conservative is to steal his wallet. Perhaps a good way to make a conservative into a liberal is to give him a welfare check.[30]

—

The research surrounding patterns of giving among the poor offers further evidence that government intervention into economic life tends to have a negative impact on charity. We saw that people who feel that it is the responsibility of the government to redistribute income are themselves less likely to give. Now we find that the beneficiaries of that redistribution are less likely to give as well.[31]

Who bears the cost when welfare policies diminish charity? We might be tempted to conclude that it is charities and the people they serve, but the impact on the nonprofit sector is minimal. Because the dollars given by the poor are relatively few, the amount of charity suppressed by welfare policies is not financially meaningful in the broad scheme of things. Consider the following rough calculation: Over the 1990s, welfare spending by federal, state, and local governments increased by about 7.5 percent per year. Of the $150 billion or so given privately during any given year in the 1990s in the United States, less than 1 percent came from welfare recipients. Each year's additional welfare spending should neutralize less than $20 million in donations by welfare recipients, or about one-hundredth of 1 percent of all private giving. Naturally, this decrease would affect different charities in different ways, so this rough calculation is not intended to say that *no* individual charity would be adversely affected, nor is it to diminish the importance of each dollar given. (This is what Mother Theresa said about work for the poor, by the poor: "We ourselves feel that what we are doing is just a drop in the ocean. But if that drop was not in the ocean, I think the ocean would be less because of that missing drop.") However, the sector as a whole would see virtually no effect from the charity not given by welfare recipients. Damage to the nonprofit sector is not a persuasive argument against welfare policies.[32]

If the money is negligible, should we care whether the non-working poor give or not? The answer is an emphatic yes because giving is about far, far more than just the money changing hands: It can be a key to a giver's own escape from poverty—although we haven't reached that part of the story yet.

Before leaving the topic of welfare and giving, here is something else to consider: If welfare discourages charity among the non-working poor, it should probably encourage charity's opposite. I have offered "voluntary sacrifice for the good of another" as an intuitive definition for charity. Aspects of "anticharity" would then include extreme selfishness, and perhaps immoral or criminal behavior.

We have already seen evidence of a connection between formal charity and other forms of moral behavior. Although eight in ten people who give money to charity "every week" said they voluntarily gave back the change mistakenly given them by a cashier in the past year, only three in ten who do not give charitably returned mistaken change. Unless we believe that (for some strange reason) cashiers make more mistakes when dealing with charitable people than when dealing with selfish people, this suggests that low giving levels are accompanied by an "ethics gap": Givers are simply more honest than nongivers.

Since welfare recipients give less than others, and giving is correlated with honesty, we might suspect that welfare receipt would have some association with unethical behavior. And indeed, many experts have argued that a tangible link exists between welfare and criminality. Citing dozens of statistical studies showing that welfare-dependent communities tend to become crime-ridden, the political scientist James Q. Wilson has identified "a failure of character" as the link between "rising welfare rolls . . . and predatory crime." This connection between crime and welfare is not obvious to all observers, though. Indeed, many academics expect rises in illegal behavior when welfare rates *fall* because falling welfare should mean more financial desperation and hence higher crime. This is what the authors of one major study in 2004 expected to find when they examined the impacts of changes to the welfare system. The authors were therefore surprised to discover that "despite participants losing their welfare benefits, both criminal activity and substance use declined over time."[33]

Selfishness, crime, and other "failures of character"—a fair summary of negative charitability—appear to be related phenomena. And welfare (at least as it was dispensed before reforms in the mid-1990s) has been implicated statistically in these failures among our most economically vulnerable citizens. This brings us back around yet again to the old favorite argument of the hard political left, that charity and compassion lie in government income redistribution. Not only do many redistributive policies—and even the mere support for these policies—displace giving, they discourage charity in recipients of redistributed income and stimulate the *opposite* of compassion.

CHAPTER 5

CHARITY BEGINS AT HOME

The family that perseveres in good works will surely have
an abundance of blessings.

CHINESE PROVERB

In 1997, a group of wealthy people, all parents of young children, sat down together in New York City to face what many of us would consider an enviable problem: How could they avoid ruining their children with all their money? Looking at wealthy friends and relatives, they saw that children who never had to work for anything often turned into lazy, uncompassionate, unhappy adults. There had to be a way to instill proper values that didn't involve getting rid of the money.

Their solution was philanthropy. With the goal of turning the threat of vice into an opportunity for virtue, the group founded the nonprofit National Center for Family Philanthropy. The Center's mission is to "promote philanthropic values, vision, and excellence across generations of donors and donor families."

It advises donors to include their children in their charitable decisionmaking and so encourage the habit of giving. According to the Center: "It's never too early to teach lessons about giving and sharing. Learning about philanthropy is the first step, practicing it and incorporating it into your family's everyday life is the second."[1]

This story might tempt one to think that family philanthropy is fine for the rich—because they have so much to give away—but is not meaningful for the rest of us. But this conclusion would be an error. We have already seen that charity is *not* just a by-product of income or wealth—it is not primarily a financial phenomenon at all. Charity is a unique and transcendent human virtue that thrives on human love. Charity is a natural family value.

Family life is connected with charity in all sorts of ways. First, at the simplest level, families are good for charity, because, except in a few situations (such as single parenthood), people who have children are more generous than people who don't. Perhaps the act of having children stimulates giving, or givers are more likely to have kids, but we find that, for example, a household with four members is more likely to give and volunteer each year than a household with only two members. Given that children are expensive and time-consuming, it is somewhat surprising that parents make available more of their time and more of their money than nonparents.[2]

Not all parents are givers, of course—some never give at all. Meanwhile, many childless adults are extremely generous. However, all else held constant, the fact of being a parent—like the fact of being religious—pushes up the likelihood of giving. If two married adults are identical in income, education, religion, race, age, and political views—but the first has one more child than the second—the odds are that the first parent will be more likely to give, and will give away significantly more dollars each year.

It stands to reason that fertility and charity are related. "Charity begins at home," wrote the Roman playwright Andria Terence. Few acts of voluntary beneficence are clearer than the unconditional care and love of a child. If one is unsatisfied with the common sense of this argument, the economic evidence makes the same point: Parenting (especially good parenting) imposes private costs on parents and creates benefits enjoyed by everyone. The private costs are explicit (basic food and shelter, education) and implicit (for example, lost career opportunities, especially for women). The benefits to society, on the other hand, include making new productive citizens who will finance public services by paying taxes, who will generate wealth and savings for investment in economies, and who will shoulder government debt. All serious studies to date tell us that the net benefits to American society from childbearing are large and positive. To assert that parenthood and money donations are positively related amounts to nothing more than saying that two types of charity are positively correlated, something that we already know is true.[3]

A second fact about charity and families: Generous parents make for generous kids. The data on this point are definitive. In one large survey from 2000, a sample of Americans was asked about their parents' volunteering, as well as their own volunteering. Among those who said they saw their parents volunteer when they were children, 56 percent grew up and volunteered every year themselves. In contrast, among people whose parents did not volunteer, only 38 percent volunteered each year as adults. This pattern held for religious and nonreligious volunteering, and persisted even when controlling for income and other differences between families. For example, if two people had the same income, education level, gender, race, and marital status—but the first had volunteer parents and the second did not—the first person was 12 points more likely to volunteer as an adult than the second.[4]

As large as this difference is between the children of generous and ungenerous parents, it becomes explosive when combined with other forces such as religion and secularism. For instance, 61 percent of adults who belonged to a house of worship in 2001, and whose parents had been volunteers, were volunteers themselves. Compare this with 44 percent of church members whose parents were not volunteers, and just 30 percent of secularists whose parents were nonvolunteers.[5]

Researchers at Indiana University came to similar conclusions in a major 2001 study of American families. The authors looked at adults who were old enough to have adult children of their own. They asked whether the current giving of the elders had an impact on the charity patterns of their children, hypothesizing that this would be evidence of a culture of charity established within that family. They found that people are much more likely to give to religious and secular causes if their parents give. Even after controlling for income, education, age, race, and many other factors that might affect giving among families, they found that increases in parental giving were associated with higher giving by their adult children.[6]

Why are the children of givers more likely to be givers themselves? Could it be that there is a "giving gene"? This proposition is less crazy than it might seem: In recent years, scholars who have studied personal characteristics such as happiness, religiosity, and innate intelligence have found a strong link to genes.[7]

That said, most of us would probably agree that charity—like good manners—is something children *learn*. And charitable parents—adults who value charity in their own lives—are the ones most likely to teach it to their kids.

Why would charitable parents want to teach their kids to give? First of all, as all givers have learned, giving makes people happy, and most parents want their children to have happy lives. Many religious parents go further: They consider it their *duty* to teach charity to their children—virtuous behavior could even be the key to the salvation of their children's souls. And perhaps there are selfish reasons, also: Parents might teach their children charity because they hope their children will remember this lesson later in life, when it is time for them to take care of their parents. Finally, there are presumably social motivations: Parents are proud when their kids are generous and embarrassed when they are selfish.

The question for most parents is how best to teach generosity to their children. Many psychologists stress the importance of teaching by example, and they believe examples are an especially effective means of teaching charity. The National Center for Family Philanthropy suggests "family giving projects" to show families how they can most effectively create these examples.[8]

Another possible way to model giving for one's children is by giving to *them*. And evidence shows that this, too, is an effective strategy. Inherited money, it turns out, stimulates charitable giving more than earned income. I have found that, among families that give charitably, inherited income raises donations by about twice as much as other forms of wealth (such as money in a savings account or the value of a house), and more than four times as much as earned income. To put this into perspective, imagine three people who are identical in their religion, level of education, race, age, and number of children. The first receives a $20,000 inheritance, the second earns $20,000 in the stock market, and the third gets a $20,000 salary increase. In the year they first receive the money, we can expect the heir to donate $82 more-to charity than he did the year before; the stock earner will give an extra $48; and the person who got the raise will give just $18 more than the year before, on average. And there is no evidence that this is due to differences in how these income and wealth sources are taxed.[9]

It may be that parents who bequeath money to their children tend to be veteran givers and have already passed this behavior on to their kids. Alternatively, it might be that people feel generous with income given to them out of generosity, or because bequests are often an unbudgeted financial windfall. Whatever the case, bequests appear to stimulate higher levels of giving in a younger generation.

Children learn charity when their parents teach it to them by their own example. But there are others ways in which parents affect a child's chances of being charitable—or not—later in life.

Perhaps not surprisingly, children are far more likely to grow up to be charitable if they are raised in a religious household. Recall that foundation executive from South Dakota, who explained why even the secular South Dakotans in my data gave such a large proportion of their incomes to charity: "We are all taught to tithe here." Indeed, this early education in giving is crucial—even if a child raised within a religious environment ultimately abandons the faith, he or she is nevertheless more likely to be charitable than a child raised in a secular household. Data show that people who were taken to church every week as children were 22 percentage points more likely to give charitably than those who were never taken to a house of worship (78 to 56 percent). This effect is evident even among those who do not attend church as adults. Secular adults who were taken to church every week as children are 21 percentage points more likely to give than those who were brought up in secular households (47 to 26 percent).[10]

Let's put this important result into perspective. Imagine two nonchurchgoers who are identical with respect to education, age, political views, and race. The only difference is that one was taken to church as a child, the other wasn't. The data tell us that the first person will be nearly twice as likely to give charitably as an adult as the second.[11]

This result is a powerful complement to the earlier findings that religious practice is the most important predictor of American charity. We saw that religious people from all walks of life and all faiths give and volunteer more for all types of charities and causes than secularists. Now we see that the gift of faith from one's parents has a large impact on generosity as an adult. With religion, it appears, parents can "hardwire" giving into their children. This might occur through the moral lessons children hear in houses of worship, or it might be from the behavioral model they see in their parents. Deeply religious people might even argue that God infuses young adherents with generosity and, no matter what their religious practices might be later, leads them to do God's work throughout their lives. All these explanations show the importance of religious faith to generosity and tie it to family life.

Marriage and divorce are also family forces we need to consider when it comes to giving. The impact of these forces on charity is more difficult to measure than the impact of religion because surveys do not generally ask people both about their current giving and whether their parents stayed married. However, we can make some logical inferences based on the earlier finding that giving parents produce giving children, and hence the family characteristics that make *parents* charitable or selfish should lead to the same outcomes among their children.

In theory, marriage should increase adult charity. There are two reasons for this. First, just pairing up should raise the likelihood of giving in a household. In a simple example, imagine a woman who has a 50 percent chance of giving to charity each year when she is single. She marries a man whose religious beliefs are similar to her own; they also have similar education levels, income, political views, and so forth. As a result, the husband also has a 50 percent chance of donating each year. When they marry, all else being equal (and assuming their giving decisions are independent), the woman's household will have a 75 percent chance of donating.[12]

Second, married people are generally a lot happier than unmarried people, and happiness is strongly associated with high levels of giving. In one recent survey, 41 percent of married people said they were "very happy," versus 26 percent of those who had never married, and only 16 percent of divorced people. In the same survey, 84 percent of "very happy people" donated to charity, versus 70 percent of "not too happy" people.[13]

Not surprisingly, given these predictions, the data are completely clear, that married adults—especially married parents—give and volunteer at far higher rates than those who are divorced or single, and this means that they provide very different models for their children. In 2002, 85 percent of married parents donated money to charity, compared with 76 percent of divorced parents, and 56 percent of single parents. Volunteering showed even greater disparities.[14]

As strong as these patterns appear, the evidence suggests that something *related* to divorce, and not simply divorce itself, causes parents to give and volunteer (or not). If we control for income, age, education, religion, political views, race, and family size, marital status itself does not strongly predict the propensity to give or volunteer. If two people who have children are identical in every way except that one person is married and the other divorced, there will not be a meaningful giving difference between the two. Divorce probably affects parental charity mostly through its connections to income, religion, happiness, and other factors I will discuss momentarily.[15]

In contrast, single parenthood is a disaster for charity. A huge and persistent giving difference exists between never-married parents and childless single people—even after correcting for income and other factors. Never-married parents are 21 percentage points less likely to give money each year than childless singles (56 to 77 percent), and also 21 points less likely to volunteer (30 to 51 percent). They are also far less likely to give in less formal ways (for example, they are less than half as likely to donate blood).

When we control for income, age, education, religion, race, and political views, the charity gap between childless singles and single parents widens. Take two identical people who have never been married, the only difference being that one has at least one child and the other has none. The single parent will be 26 percentage points less likely to give each year, on average, than the childless person even though they have the same income, education, religion, and so on.

The 26-point giving difference between single parents and childless single people probably *underestimates* the effects of illegitimacy because the data do not allow us to distinguish between children born to truly single parents and those born to stable cohabiting heterosexual or homosexual couples—couples that most likely give at higher rates than mothers who have no partner living in the household. So a charitable lesbian mother in a stable partnership "looks" in the data like an unusually charitable single mother, whereas she is not single in any meaningful sense. The evidence does not exist to suggest that these nontraditional parents are uncharitable, or that they teach their children to be selfish. We know that broken homes and poor parenting are terrible for charity. And we know that strong families are good for charity. There is no evidence, however, that the *nature* of that family—heterosexual or same-sex parents—matters.

Why don't single parents give as much as married parents or childless singles? One straightforward explanation for low giving by single parents was introduced in the chapter on welfare. Single parenthood is a major predictor of welfare receipt because households usually have a division of labor; it is difficult to raise children and pursue a productive career simultaneously. Couples can solve this problem when one parent is a principal earner and the other is a principal caregiver. Single parents frequently resort to welfare to make childcare and economic ends meet. And as we have seen, people who receive welfare are much less likely to give to charity than people who don't.[16]

I have already noted that there are no data explicitly linking the marital status of one's parents to one's own charity later in life. But there is plenty of evidence that divorce and single parenthood have a huge impact on children's overall socialization. Children from broken homes have more social problems and are less likely to be successful in life than children from intact families. And this would certainly suppress their giving behavior.

Some things we know for sure when it comes to broken families and their impact on childhood development. First, *fathers matter* in raising responsible, nondelinquent children. Many studies have uncovered strong links between antisocial behavior and family breakdown—and especially a lack of fathers with honest jobs who live at home with their children and wives. Children who grow up without fathers are more likely to fail in school or drop out before graduating from high school, to have emotional or psychological problems, to engage in early sexual activity, to become pregnant, and to have problems with drugs and alcohol. Seventy percent of juvenile delinquents currently in custody were raised without their biological fathers. Young men in this group are seven times more likely to end up in prison than those from stable families. Given the established links between selfishness and other antisocial behaviors, it is almost certainly true that absent fathers have a negative impact on their offspring's charity.[17]

Researchers have found that divorce followed by remarriage is not a good substitute for once-married parents in their children's success. For example, stepchildren (90 percent of whom live with a biological mother and a stepfather) are much more likely than biological children to suffer from child abuse, neglect, and lack of supervision—even after correcting for differences in family income and other circumstances. Stepchildren are also more likely than children living with both biological parents to drop out of school and become pregnant as teenagers. It would be naïve to assume that the net indirect effects of divorce on most children's learned charitability would not be negative.[18]

Statistically, it is nearly impossible to disentangle welfare, single parenting, and antisocial behavior—including selfishness. These phenomena are grave enough by themselves, because poverty and selfishness reinforce each other in a vicious cycle. But this link is especially disturbing because we now have evidence that parental generosity (or selfishness) is a root cause of children's giving (or selfishness). In other words, the vicious cycle runs not just through people's lives, but also through generations of families.

⌒

Given what we know about teaching charity within families, when is the best time to do so? Child psychologists suggest that it is best to teach most positive (or negative) social behaviors when a child is in elementary school; this is therefore probably the best time to teach charitable behavior as well. Several philanthropic foundations and academic researchers taking this point seriously have started an initiative called *Learning to Give*. This initiative aims to teach—and help parents to teach—school children to be givers for the rest of their lives. With the assistance of child development experts and scholars in philanthropy, the initiative has developed a set of strategies—such as family giving projects in the community—to inculcate giving habits among the very young.[19]

Explicit strategies to teach kids to give are sensible, and usually even intuitive—but for several reasons they are much more easily executed in some kinds of families than in others. First, happy, intact families tend to possess the best parenting skills. A great volume of research has shown that adults in happy relationships tend to be far more effective parents than those in unstable, unhappy relationships. Second, married parents are most likely to participate all together in family projects of all kinds, including giving projects. Finally, as many writers have shown, intact families are far more likely than broken or single-parent families to be integrated into their communities. This is especially true among religious families, which have built-in community groups in their houses of worship.[20]

⌒

The family characteristics that predict charitable giving among parents and children help illuminate the giving differences between political conservatives and liberals. People on the political right are more likely than those on the left to exhibit the family patterns—such as religious participation and stable marriage—that lead parents and their children toward charitable giving.

We have already established the link between religion and politics: A self-identified conservative is almost twice as likely to attend his or her house of worship weekly as a self-described liberal, and a liberal is nearly twice as likely as a conservative never to attend. Therefore, liberals are less likely than conservatives to put their children in a religious environment that is almost singularly conducive to charitable giving for both the parents, and the children themselves when they grow to adulthood. Conservatives are also far more likely to be married than liberals: 16 percentage points more likely in 2002.[21]

Liberals have fewer children than conservatives, which means that they are less likely to give and volunteer (because people with more children donate more time and money than those with fewer, even after correcting for income). Having fewer kids also means that charitable liberals pass on their charity—as well as their political views—to fewer people. To illustrate the point, consider this: In 2002, if you had randomly selected one hundred politically conservative adults in America (none from the same families), you would have found, between them, 212 children. If you had selected a hundred liberal adults, they would have had 156 children. This gap is primarily caused by religious differences and marriage patterns.[22]

Low liberal fertility may represent something more fundamental about liberal charity as well. In a developed nation such as the United States, the economic incentives to have children fall when people no longer "need" them for support in old age. The decision to have children becomes more and more one of focusing on others (one's children and society) rather than on oneself. It is the charity decision in a nutshell. Some might argue (or at least, they might privately believe) that the decision to forgo childbearing is a sign of selfishness, particularly in an economic environment in which per capita personal income is rising.

Happiness is another factor that explains the relationship between politics and charity. American conservatives consistently report higher levels of subjective well-being than liberals. For example, conservatives in 2002 were 30 percent more likely than liberals to say they were "very happy" in their lives, and 36 percent less likely to say they were "not too happy." This is partly—but not entirely—a result of life circumstances, such as income, education, race, or gender. Controlling for income, education, age, race, gender, religion, and children, conservatives are, on average, 7.5 percentage points more likely than liberals to say they are very happy. In a later chapter, I will show that happiness strongly predicts how likely one is to give to charity—and thereby teach charitable behavior to the next generation.[23]

Why are conservatives happier than liberals? American conservatives over the past few years have had more to be happy about in national politics—I have a lot of grumpy liberal friends—although everyone knows that the fortunes of the Republican Party will inevitably reverse: They may as soon as 2006. And the data I've drawn on to demonstrate the correlation between happiness and politics is from 2000—when a Democrat was still in the White House. Besides, it is hard to imagine that the president's political party or the make-up of the Senate would *dominate* the happiness of more than a handful of emotionally precarious political activists.

A more likely explanation goes back to families: Conservatives tend to enjoy more traditional, religious, and stable families than liberals; these types of families bring ongoing happiness for most people. It is not controversial to point out that secularism and single parenthood are more common among liberals than conservatives, and many liberals would not even say that this is a pity: Secular humanism and the emancipation from the obligation to marry have both been parts of the personal liberation—especially of women—celebrated by the left. In contrast, conservatives have fought these trends all along, and they experience these phenomena far less frequently as a result. Thoughtful people will always disagree about whether secularism and having children outside of marriage are always and everywhere bad things, but no reasonable person believes they bring no costs whatsoever. Less happiness and the resulting effects on charity are two of these costs.

The evidence on children and charity has significant implications for public policy. One effective technique parents can use to model giving behavior for their kids is to give them an inheritance. Since inherited money stimulates charity among heirs, bequests are more than just monetary gifts—they are a means to make one's heirs more charitable. What does all this imply about the hotly debated inheritance tax in America?

The tax on inherited income—also known as the estate tax or, pejoratively, as the "death tax"—has always been divisive. Some support it because it is a handy income source in the United States. For example, the liberal lobbying group *United for a Fair Economy* estimates that in 2003 the estate tax provided $20 billion for the U.S. Treasury. It is also fodder for class conflict in politics because only the wealthiest American families leave bequests of significant size for their heirs. Many economists object to the estate tax because it tends to penalize savings and so affect long-term economic growth and investment. It is also unfair in the view of many people because it is a "double tax"—most money in estates was taxed when it was earned and is taxed a second time when passed on to heirs. At present, liberals tend to favor maintaining or increasing the estate tax, but conservatives would prefer to lower or eliminate it.[24]

Charities are concerned about efforts to lower or discontinue the estate tax because many people avoid the tax by bequeathing tax-deductible donations to nonprofit organizations. How much would eliminating the estate tax affect charitable donations? A lot, some people believe. For example, a Congressional Budget Office estimate from 2001 noted that a 10 percent decrease in the estate tax rates would stimulate a decrease in charitable bequests of about 4.2 percent. What if the estate tax should be eliminated altogether? Charitable bequests came to about $19.8 billion in 2004. Given that this tax affected about 58 percent of all estate income in 2005, the cost of repealing it from its top

2006 rate of 46 percent to zero would be about $8 billion less in donations to charities each year.[25]

Not surprisingly, then, much of the American nonprofit sector has been opposed to abolishing or lowering the estate tax. It has a difficult case to make to the public, however. The argument is basically this: "Our organization supports the estate tax so that you and your family will continue to try and avoid it by giving us money." This is as self-interested as an accounting firm that might argue for a pointlessly complicated tax code to ensure more income for preparing people's tax returns.

My estimate of $8 billion in lost donations is liberal. Many experts believe that the loss would be much lower, and some even predict that charitable giving would *increase* if the tax were repealed. One noted scholar on wealth transfers between generations writes that "repealing [the estate tax] would lead to greater national and personal economic growth, encourage charitable giving to be more of a voluntary act than one spurred by tax incentives, and mobilize for charity the increasing affluence and philanthropic inclinations of many Americans."[26]

Further, as we have seen, even if the estate tax's demise did redirect donations toward heirs, these heirs would be especially likely to give much of it away. This is an important point for today's working-age professionals, who stand to receive the bulk of the more than $50 trillion that researchers on intergenerational wealth expect to be transferred between now and the middle of the century. Repealing the estate tax would stimulate about $1 billion per year in new giving by heirs.[27]

One more point about the estate tax: Since it is a major income redistribution mechanism, we can probably predict as much about the giving by *supporters* of the tax as we can about those *affected* by it. People who believe the government should take part of my gift to my own child—to use the money for purposes deemed more important by government officials—are less likely to be givers themselves than people who oppose the tax. This prediction is based on the fact that supporting forced income redistribution suppresses private giving, and on the evidence that charity and economic liberty are mutually reinforcing virtues.

Charity is not a good reason to oppose the abolition of the estate tax. On the contrary, repealing the tax would allow parents to model charitable giving through bequests and to provide heirs with an opportunity to give when they receive these bequests. Furthermore, the estate tax abridges one's freedom to give one's honestly earned money—much of which has already been taxed—to whomever one wants. Like any other kind of forced income redistribution, this abridgment is inconsistent with charitable attitudes and behavior. And if the tax is intended merely to protect nonprofit organizations' giving base, it treats charity as nothing more than any other type of financial transaction.

⌐

At this point, we have firmly established the forces of charity: religion, skepticism about the government in economic life, work, and strong families. We are closer now to the true reasons conservatives are more personally charitable than liberals.

Before exploring further the implications for American politics, we need to answer two questions. First, do these forces also explain charity differences between countries? Second, why do charity differences matter?

CHAPTER 6

CONTINENTAL DRIFT

The Sea of Faith
Was once, too, at the full, and round earth's shore
Lay like the folds of a bright girdle furl'd.
But now I only hear
Its melancholy, long, withdrawing roar,
Retreating, to the breath
Of the night-wind, down the vast edges drear
And naked shingles of the world.

MATTHEW ARNOLD, "DOVER BEACH" (1867)[1]

On December 26, 2004, the most powerful earthquake in forty years (9.0 on the Richter scale) struck the floor of the Indian Ocean, off the coast of the Indonesian island of Sumatra. Within minutes, a series of tidal waves radiated from the epicenter. The waves were a hundred miles long from crest to crest, and sped at five hundred miles an hour toward land. Within fifteen minutes, the western coast of Sumatra was engulfed. Entire villages were wiped out—in some areas, the waves killed 70 percent of the inhabitants. In an hour and a half, the waves reached Thailand; in two hours, Sri Lanka and India. The monster waves created destruction as far away as the eastern coast of Africa. The disaster's toll was astronomical: Three months after the tragedy, more than 300,000 people in eleven countries were dead or missing. Hundreds of thousands lost their livelihoods, and millions were made homeless.

Although the disaster struck halfway around the world, the outpouring of American aid was tremendous. This generosity might have surprised Adam Smith, the father of modern capitalism. In his classic 1759 treatise, *The Theory of Moral Sentiments,* he maintained that people cannot be expected to care much about those who are far away:

> Let us suppose that the great empire of China, with all its myriads of inhabitants, was suddenly swallowed up by an earthquake, and let us consider how a man of humanity in Europe, who had no sort of connexion with that part of the world, would be affected upon receiving intelligence of this dreadful calamity. . . . If he was to lose his little finger to-morrow, he would not sleep to-night; but, provided he never saw [the Chinese people killed by an earthquake], he will snore with the most profound security over the ruin of a hundred millions of his brethren, and the destruction of that immense multitude seems plainly an object less interesting to him, than this paltry misfortune of his own.[2]

The film director Mel Brooks puts the idea more succinctly: "Tragedy is when I cut my finger. Comedy is when you fall into an open sewer and die."

And yet nations and individuals around the world rallied in unprecedented numbers to contribute to disaster relief efforts. Charities in the affected countries were deluged with hundreds of millions of dollars in cash and supplies from governments, corporations, foundations, and individuals. By the middle of March 2005, the World Food Program, sponsored by the United Nations, had distributed more than a quarter of a billion dollars in aid to disaster victims. This much or more had been pledged as well by the governments of many developed countries, including Germany ($674 million), Australia ($380 million), Japan ($500 million), and the United States ($350 million).[3]

In the United States, the majority of aid came from private citizens—individual contributions outstripped the government aid by almost three to one. Six months after the disaster, Americans had donated more than $1.5 billion in cash and gifts. The American Red Cross alone collected private tsunami donations adding up to nearly $400 million by the middle of March 2005. Catholic Relief Services collected nearly $100 million, and Oxfam America $30 million. Private contributions from the United States were so prolific that they created spending bottlenecks for some charities. Doctors Without Borders, for example, stopped accepting gifts just two weeks after the tragedy because it was unable to absorb and spend the donations it was receiving.[4]

America was nevertheless criticized for the inadequacy of its aid efforts. Many critics of the Bush administration—both in America and in Europe—noted that the most generous of governments (Germany) pledged nearly twice as much in assistance as the U.S. government. The executive director of the liberal National Committee for Responsive Philanthropy (NCRP) saw this as a personal charitable failing of the president: "President Bush took an embarrassingly long time to show any personal interest or concern for the victims and survivors of the greatest natural disaster of modern times . . . the U.S. government aid commitment . . . pales against the commitments of other smaller and less wealthy nations."[5]

The most famous criticism, though, came from Jan Egeland, the United Nations emergency relief coordinator, who was widely reported to have called American relief efforts "stingy." American leaders sensitive to the stereotype of American selfishness came down hard on Egeland. President Bush said that Egeland was "misguided and ill-informed." Secretary of State Colin Powell responded as well: "The United States is not stingy. We are the greatest contributor to international relief efforts in the world."[6]

But Egeland had been misquoted and misinterpreted. His full statement was this: "Christmas time should remind many Western countries at least how rich we have become, and if actually the foreign assistance of many countries now is 0.1 or 0.2 percent of their gross national income, I think that is stingy really." In fact, Egeland was not criticizing American tsunami aid specifically; rather, he was indirectly repeating what has become a mantra in Europe about what is wrong with official American foreign aid in general: It does not rise to the level of *0.7 percent* of U.S. GDP.

Where does this "0.7 percent" figure come from? In 1992, a cross-section of representatives of the world's nations adopted a plan for action under the administration of the United Nations, which they called Agenda 21. This plan included a government foreign aid target of 0.7 percent of GDP for the most developed nations, including Western Europe and the United States. Agenda 21 soon became a stick used by the international press and world leaders to flog the United States, which (although by far the world's largest donor nation in dollars) has a foreign aid budget that is only a fraction of the 0.7 percent target. For more than a decade, assorted critics of the United States have used the 0.7 goal as incontrovertible proof that America is selfish. In the words of Clare Short, Britain's International Development Secretary until 2003, the United States is "turning its back on the needy of the world" by failing to meet the 0.7 target.[7]

The problem with this criticism is that it fails to take into account the disproportionately high level of private charity in the United States. How much does direct government foreign aid understate true American humanitarian assistance? A lot, according to the United States Agency for International Development, which decisively denounced the common European attack on American generosity in a 2002 report. It is true that U.S. official development assistance (ODA), at about $10 billion, is only about a tenth of 1 percent of GDP. "However, this amount is accompanied annually by about $13 billion in other types of government assistance, and about $16 billion from private sources, including foundations, religious congregations, voluntary organizations, universities, and corporations."[8]

Furthermore, American private giving for international aid is only a tiny fraction of the total picture of U.S. private generosity: only about 2 percent of all American charitable giving. Far more money goes to domestic causes in education, health, human services, the environment, the arts, and religion.

Why do Europeans persist in their criticisms of American generosity? One reason is that giving at the private level is a foreign concept to them.

There is so little private charity in Europe that it is difficult to find information on the subject—so irrelevant is it that few researchers have even bothered to investigate it recently. The best data on private money donations in Europe are from the late 1990s. These data, however, show a huge charity gap that we can be confident has grown only in the intervening decade (for reasons I will discuss in a moment). Specifically, no Western European population comes remotely close the United States in per capita private charity. The closest nation, Spain, has average giving that is less than half that of the United States. Per person, Americans give three and a half times as much as the French, seven times as much as the Germans, and fourteen times as much as the Italians.[9]

As interesting as this comparison is, it might not be a fair one because average incomes vary between countries quite a bit, as do the prices of goods and services. For example, it would not be realistic to expect a person in Ireland—where an average annual income is $22,000—to give as much per year as an American, whose income on average is more than 50 percent higher. But when we correct for average income, the results barely change. Even accounting for differences in standard of living, Americans give more than twice as high a percentage of their incomes to charity as the Dutch, almost three times as much as the French, more than five times as much as the Germans, and more than ten times as much as the Italians.[10]

Americans give at much higher levels and rates than people in practically any other part of the world—not just Western Europe. When we consider other nations, America looks better and better, but Western Europe looks worse and worse: In 1995, Tanzanians gave a larger part of their incomes than Norwegians.

Kenyans gave more than Austrians and Germans. And almost everybody—Africans, South Americans, Eastern Europeans—gave more than Italians.[11]

What about gifts of time? How does the United States compare to Western Europe in the tendency to volunteer charitably? Does this erase the trans-Atlantic charity gap?

No. Data from 1998 on whether people in America and Western Europe volunteer for religious, political, and charitable causes show that the story is the same. As for money donations, no European country reaches American volunteering levels—indeed, most don't even come remotely close. For example, Americans are 15 percentage points more likely to volunteer than the Dutch (51 to 36 percent), 21 points more likely than the Swiss, and 32 points more likely than the Germans (fewer than one in five of which volunteer for any charities, churches, or other causes). These volunteering differences are not attributable to the average level of education or income. On the contrary, if we look at two people who are identical in age, sex, marital status, education, and real income—but one is European and the other American—the probability is far lower that the European will volunteer than the American. For example, an Austrian who "looks" just like an American will be 32 percentage points less likely to volunteer, a Spaniard will be 31 points less likely, and an Italian will be 29 points less likely.[12]

It is clear that the stereotype of stingy Americans just doesn't hold up. The American government is not the only giver. When we look at the overall charity of Americans, we see that by international standards we are an extraordinarily generous nation.

I was wary when I first began to look at data comparing Americans and Europeans because people in different countries answer survey questions about money in different ways. If you ask an American how much money he or she earns you get an annual, pre-tax figure. A Spaniard, on the other hand, will give you the amount he or she takes home each month, after taxes. It stands to reason that different populations should respond to questions about charity in non-comparable ways as well. Maybe what we consider giving in America is not thought of as such in, say, France—and thereby we have an artificial impression of low charity there.

I vetted my statistics with some of my European colleagues. On a trip to Russia, I showed shockingly low Russian average volunteering rates to a professor of nongovernmental studies at a Moscow university: "No, that can't possibly be right," he said. But then he surprised me: "There is no way that such a high percentage of Russians actually volunteer each year. You are overestimating Russian voluntarism, because Russians overstate their charitable activities." And this was the same reaction about reported giving and volunteering levels that I got from colleagues in other European countries.[13]

But my Russian friend did bring up two explanations that are the most common European justifications for the transatlantic charity gap.

First, many Europeans argue that their high taxes, which provide revenues to generous social welfare systems, pay for much of what Americans cover with private charity. This is a product of European social consensus, the argument goes, making it no less "charitable" than private giving. Furthermore, many believe, the state is more effective and dependable for providing support for public services and relief to the needy than reliance on voluntary sources of aid.

One technical problem arises with this argument: The average tax burden in all European countries is *not* higher than it is in the United States. A British family, for instance, relinquishes an average of 10.8 percent of its household income to the government in income taxes. This is *lower* than what an average American family pays—11.3 percent.[14]

Still, the social spending argument is undeniably strong. A conversation with, say, a middle-class Norwegian is sufficient to convince any skeptic that high taxes and generous social welfare benefits are indeed part of a social consensus in modern Europe. This by itself separates the income redistribution arguments of Europeans from those of American liberals. In the United States, opinions about redistribution are generally not backed up by policies. Furthermore, there is no American consensus on high levels of social spending. Thus, though the "charity through government spending" argument is not a legitimate defense for failing to give in America, it might be in Europe.

Social consensus, however, is not the same thing as unanimity. Undoubtedly, forced taxes are paid against the will of many Europeans—and Europe has the tax evasion to prove it: "Massive tax evasion is Europe's dirty little secret" declared the *Wall Street Journal Europe* recently. Estimates suggest that Europe's underground economy (illegally untaxed) is nearly twice that of America's. This does not mean that social welfare spending is bad policy, just that it is not a *voluntary sacrifice* for many Europeans; European government spending therefore cannot be viewed as anything equivalent to private giving.[15]

The second justification we often hear from Europeans is that Americans give more because our tax system creates incentives to be charitable. The American federal and state governments provide tax deductions in exchange for charitable contributions, meaning that there is considerably more government involvement in "charity" than meets the eye. According to this argument, true American private charity is probably not much higher than European private giving.

This argument is wrong. First, American tax deductions represent only about 20 percent of the total value of U.S. private charity. This is nowhere near the size of the gap in average giving between the United States and the European nations. For example, even if we erase 20 percent of American gifts, the average American still gives five and a half times as much money to charity each year as the average German. Second, many European countries have tax incentives similar to (or more generous than) those in the United States. Third, this argument pertains only to money donations, but nonmoney giving in Europe is much lower than in the United States as well. Fourth, tax deductions do not drive the vast majority of private donations in America.

Why is Europe so uncharitable? For many of the same reasons, it turns out, that uncharitable Americans are. We saw that Americans are relatively unlikely to behave charitably if they are nonreligious, believe that it is the government's job to redistribute income, and suffer from unstable family conditions. There is ample evidence that each of these forces is stronger in Europe than in America, and that these forces suppress charitable giving more in Europe than they do here.

Let's begin with religion in Europe—or more accurately, the lack of it. The most diplomatic way to describe the status of religion in Europe is to say that the Continent is "post-Christian." Europeans may have some cultural memory of Christianity, but few practice, and many are openly hostile to their religious patrimony. Charity in Europe has suffered as a result.

Recently, the head of a major European think tank summarized the differences between Europe and America: "The biblical references in politics, the division of the world between good and evil, these are things that [Europeans] simply don't get. In a number of areas, it seems to me that we are no longer part of the same civilization." According to a former advisor to François Mitterand, the late French president, "Europe defends a secular vision of the world. It does not separate matters of urgency from long-term considerations. The United States compensates for its shortsightedness, its tendency to improvise, with an altogether biblical self-assurance in its transcendent destiny."[16]

Europe and America are undeniably drifting apart culturally, especially in attitudes toward religious faith. With the exception of Ireland, the percentage of the population that says it has no religion or that it never attends a house of worship is higher in every European country than it is in the United States, and the percentage that goes to church every week is lower. The differences are dramatic. For example, a British citizen in 2002 was three times as likely to be completely secular as an American (63 to 19 percent), and one third as likely to be religious (13 to 37 percent). In Holland, 9 percent of the population attends church regularly; in France, 7 percent; and in Norway, 4 percent. European secularism is also more aggressive than American secularism. It is one thing to neglect religion; it is another thing entirely to disdain it openly. Yet Europeans are far more likely than Americans to do precisely this. For example, in 1998, 40 percent of Swedes and 40 percent of Norwegians "strongly agreed" with this statement: "Looking at the world, religions bring more conflict than peace." Similarly, 28 percent of Italians and British held this strong antireligious view. In contrast, only 8 percent of Americans felt this way.[17]

Secularism correlates directly with low rates of charity in Europe, just as it does in the United States. All across Europe, religious citizens are more than twice as likely to volunteer for charities and causes as secularists. This correlation is specifically tied to religion, not some other characteristic associated with it. For example, imagine two Europeans—one typical secularist and one lonely churchgoer—who are identical with respect to education, income, age, marital status, and gender. The churchgoer would be 30 percentage points more likely than the secularist to volunteer each year, and 15 points more likely to volunteer for explicitly nonreligious charities. In some countries, the disparity is much larger. Consider France: In 1998, 73 percent of the population were secularists. The odd French churchgoer was 54 percentage points more likely than a demographically identical secularist to volunteer, and 25 points more likely to volunteer for secular causes. Similarly, a religious British person would be 43 points more likely to volunteer than a demographically identical British secularist (and 24 points more likely for nonreligious causes).[18]

The impact of being European *and* secular makes the difference explode. Imagine comparing secular Frenchmen with religious Americans who are identical with respect to education, age, income, sex, and marital status. We can predict that 27 percent of the secular French will volunteer, compared with 83 percent of the religious Americans.[19]

What explains the high levels of European secularism? Some argue that it is the suspicion Europeans have about religion after centuries of religion-related wars. Others see it as simply a self-fulfilling prophecy from European humanist intellectuals, who have always seen doom for organized religion as a symbol of social progress. This idea goes back more than a century, and is characteristic of the social theories of Central Europe. Karl Marx famously referred to religion as the "opiate of the masses," and believed it was doomed to extinction as societies progressed. Sigmund Freud and Auguste Comte viewed religion as akin to mental illness or as a manifestation of superstition. Whatever the reason for Europe's rapid secularization, it is a fact. In the words of Pope Benedict XVI, "Europe has developed a culture which, in a way never before known to humanity, excludes God from public conscience." He reached this conclusion with sadness, but for many Europeans today it is a major victory.[20]

America is as much a part of the Western world as Europe, of course. So why hasn't American religion withered in a similar way? Indeed, data on religious participation show an increase in church membership over the past two centuries—from 17 percent of the population at the time of the American Revolution to a third of the population at the time of the Civil War, to about 60 percent today. It may be that the lack of an official government religion in America, leading to a highly competitive market for souls, has kept religion in touch with the needs of American worshippers. And America's sunny resistance to the hold of depressing European social theories may have helped provide a defense against the creep of secularism. Whatever the reason, there is no indication that the forces of American secularism are a political or social threat on any European scale, at least not yet. American charities can thank God that this is so.[21]

Some experts argue that European secularism revolves not around faith but stems from European leftist politics. The collapse of Soviet communism in 1989, and therefore of a legitimate alternative to capitalism, was a major blow to many Western European intellectuals, who reacted strongly against the forces responsible for exposing communism's moral unacceptability and economic untenability. A major force here was the United States, which may partly explain the nearly hardwired resentment against America among European elites. But the Catholic Church also played a major role in the fall of communism. Pope John Paul II was responsible in no small part for the mobilization of Poles and other Eastern Europeans against their Communist leaders—an achievement that earned the Holy Father the permanent enmity of many European leftists.

Ongoing leftist political sympathies—with accompanying secularism—also lurk behind the low levels of European charity. Recently, I was teaching a class in Moscow for Russian university students of nonprofit management. After reviewing the data on low levels of giving and volunteering in Russia, I asked the students why they believed this was so. Their answers were immediate and unanimous. "Our parents," one student told me, "don't have any religion, and believe the government should provide for all of people's basic needs."

Beyond anecdotes, however, there is plenty of empirical evidence that makes the same point. Recall that American proponents of income redistribution are personally far less charitable than opponents of redistribution, even after correcting for income, race, education, and other personal differences. And Europeans are far more supportive of economic redistribution than their American counterparts. When Europeans and Americans were presented with the statement "The government has a responsibility to reduce income inequality," only 33 percent of Americans agreed—far fewer than the level in any European nation. For example, in Spain, 77 percent favored greater redistribution; in Italy, 65 percent; and in Germany, 49 percent. The level of agreement with this statement correlated consistently with national charity rates. So, for example, in Spain, 13 percent volunteered for nonreligious charities; in Italy, it was 11 percent; and in Germany, 10 percent. Considering 22 Eastern and Western European countries together, a 10 percent increase in the percentage of the population that believes the government has a responsibility to reduce income inequality is associated with a 6 percent decrease in the percentage volunteering for nonreligious causes, and a 5 percent decrease in religious volunteering.[22]

What explains the high levels of collectivist sentiment in Europe? To begin with, income redistribution is a core tenet of left-wing politics, and the percentage of the population that classifies itself as "left" or "far left" politically is much higher in Europe than in the United States. European political parties that cater to collectivist tastes thus wield considerable power. In most of Western Europe, this includes parties with radical redistributive platforms. For example, the 2002 legislative elections in France featured six Trotskyite, or Communist, parties, which each won at least 1 percent of the popular vote—in addition to the Socialist Party, which won nearly 25 percent of the vote. All told, the French hard left (which does not include the socialists, who would be "hard left" by American standards) garnered about 14 percent. French politics also includes the peculiar presence of the extreme right, most notably in the form of Jean-Marie Le Pen's National Front, which won 11 percent of the votes in the legislative election (and 17 percent in the first round of the 2002 presidential election). The National Front is as unsympathetic to the free-market distribution of resources as the Communists—indeed, the National Front and the communists *both* find their strongest support among factory workers and the unemployed.

All told, a majority of French voters voted in 2002 for parties that explicitly favor punitive forced redistribution. The statistics are similar in recent elections in Italy, Spain, and most other European countries.[23]

Even where the radical left does not wield political power, softer socialist parties still capture a significant part of the electorate. Much of Western Europe has lived under socialist and social democratic regimes for most of the past fifty years. Why is this, when these kinds of political movements are so conspicuously absent in the United States? Gallons of ink have been spilled explaining why apparently similar cultures in the United States and Europe are so ideologically different. Robert Kagan sums up the difference when he says, "Americans are from Mars and Europeans are from Venus: They agree on little and understand one another less and less."[24]

Whatever the explanation, the regimes in European countries have almost certainly accustomed people of average and modest means to their inalienable right to the incomes of more prosperous citizens. People will always disagree about whether income-leveling policies in Europe are wise, and whether redistributive sentiments are healthy. It appears beyond dispute, however, that the widespread will to redistribute income comes at a significant cost for European private charity, just as it does in certain parts of the American population.

"Europe as we know it is slowly going out of business," wrote a *Washington Post* columnist in 2005. The writer was making a point about demography, not economics: Europe's low birthrate has been shrinking its native populations for more than two decades. At current birthrate levels, Germany is poised to lose the equivalent of the former East Germany's entire population by 2050, and Spain's population will shrink by one quarter over the same period. By mid-century, more than half of Italians will have no sisters or brothers, no cousins, and no aunts or uncles. Since the end of World War II, every European country has decreased its birthrate—most have done so radically—to the point that today, no country in the European Union has a birthrate that even approaches the population replacement level. One has to go back seven centuries to the black plague to find a time when Europe's population declined as quickly as it is declining today.[25]

A replacement fertility level—meaning that a population stays constant because as many people are born as die each year—in the developed world is about 2.1 children born to each woman. In 2005, this was almost exactly the average number of children born to women in the United States. In stark contrast, the European Union has a birthrate of 1.5 children per woman. In France, the number is 1.8; in Britain, 1.7; and in formerly Catholic Italy and Spain, 1.3. In Germany, where the number of children per woman is currently 1.4, the most recent data tell us that 30 percent of German women are—and will remain— childless.[26]

Why have so many Europeans stopped having children? A United Nations policy paper from 2000 identified as culprits falling marriage rates, rising unmarried cohabitation by couples, and rising divorce. The report notes that at least 90 percent of Swedish women currently cohabit before—or instead of—marriage, and at least 40 percent of today's young Swedes will never marry. Or consider that, although 53 percent of British men were married in 2003, only 42 percent will be married by 2031; most will choose cohabitation (or multiple cohabitations) instead.[27]

Modern European attitudes about family life are not just nontraditional; they are antitraditional. In 2002, 55 percent of Spaniards disagreed that it is best to marry if one wants to have children (versus 19 percent of Americans). And 81 percent agreed that divorce is the best solution for couples who can't seem to work out their marital problems (versus 43 percent of Americans).[28]

Europe's empty baby carriages are not new news. In 1982, the German novelist Günter Grass wrote *Headbirths: Or the Germans Are Dying Out,* which featured a young German "model couple" who travel instead of bothering with children. "They keep a cat," Grass writes, in ironic summary.[29]

Just as charity begins at home less and less frequently in Europe in the decision to have children, so does the broader decision to remain childless become part of the decision not to help others. As in America, there is evidence that childless Europeans are less likely to donate to charity than those with kids. In some countries, the effect of children on giving is strong; in others, it is weak—but it is always positive, and independent of forces such as income and education. For example, imagine two French couples who resemble each other in income, age, education, and even religious participation—the only difference is that the first couple has two children, the other none. The first couple will be 33 percent more likely to volunteer for charity than the second. The demographic implosion of Europe lies in some part behind its low charitable giving and volunteering rates.[30]

Charity is not the only casualty of Europe's population slide—the effects of current childlessness on the European economy are a disaster in the making. Europe as a region already has the highest proportion of elderly people in the world: Fifteen percent of the population is sixty-five years or older—and that percentage is expected to double by 2050. Europe's creaky pension systems are known by economists as "pay-as-you-go," meaning that current pensions are paid out of the wages of current workers. Solvency of this system as the population ages—and new workers are not there to pay retirees' pensions—almost certainly means that Europeans face at least one of three scenarios: dramatically lower pension benefits, impossibly high taxes, or uncontrolled immigration. In short, Europe's demographic crater leaves its people with a set of unpalatable choices, economic problems, and even lower means to give charitably.[31]

—◦—

To some, the trend of much of the developed world—especially Western Europe—toward a secular, statist, low-fertility culture is natural, probably inevitable, and maybe even desirable. It is true that European social welfare systems are effective in providing an economic floor for the citizens of these countries (for the moment), that poor Americans are poorer than poor Europeans, and that income inequality is much lower in Western Europe than it is in the United States. It would be foolish to deny that there are many benefits to these systems, which are as popular among average Europeans as the American system is in the United States.

But much about these systems does not appear to encourage healthy societies in the long run. The most obvious symptoms of this are economic. We have already discussed the effects of the European "baby bust" on the financing of pension systems, but the economic maladies go deeper than just this. According to the Organisation for Economic Co-operation and Development (OECD), the United States experienced real economic growth that was about 60 percent higher than the European Union's over the period from 2000 to 2004. The OECD's chief economist argues that, in twenty years, the average U.S. citizen will be twice as rich as the average Frenchman or German. According to one large international financial services company in a briefing for its clients, "The U.S.'s GDP growth rates when it was in a 'recession' would be an almost boom condition in Europe." And a 2004 report from a Swedish think tank notes that France, Italy, Great Britain, and Germany have lower GDP per capita than forty-six American states. The authors of this report note that today, 40 percent of Swedish households would be considered low-income in the United States.[32]

My European friends have told me many times that differences in per capita income and economic growth might seem a small price to pay for a high quality of life brought about by economic security and low inequality. In other words, Europeans may be a little poorer than Americans, but much happier, on average. These claims, however, do not square with the facts. Consider the differences between European and American populations in subjective well-being—that is, self-judged happiness. In 2002, Europeans and Americans were asked, "If you were to consider your life in general, how happy or unhappy would you say you are, on the whole?" A greater percentage of Americans (56 percent) answered "completely happy" or "very happy" than people in European countries. For example, the percentage was 36 percent in Spain and Holland, 35 percent in France, and 31 percent in Germany. It was even lower in Eastern Europe. It appears that something is missing for many Europeans.[33]

I am convinced that this "something"—or at least part of this something—is personal generosity, as reflected in giving, volunteering, and even parenting. The next chapter lays out the evidence for this claim. I will show why a lack of private charity probably lurks behind the relative unhappiness and disappointing economic growth in Europe—and poses a threat to America as well.

CHAPTER 7

CHARITY MAKES YOU HEALTHY, HAPPY, AND RICH

It is one of the most beautiful compensations of this life that no man can sincerely try to help another without helping himself. . . . Serve and thou shall be served.
RALPH WALDO EMERSON

"God gave me my money," said John D. Rockefeller, the American billionaire and philanthropist, in 1905. This is probably the most commonly misunderstood quotation attributed to the man. To someone negatively disposed to Rockefeller—because of his business practices or wealth itself—"God gave me my money" sounds like an outrageous justification for one man's hoarding enormous personal wealth and enjoying an opulent lifestyle in the midst of poverty he felt he had no duty to alleviate. However, this is precisely the opposite of what Rockefeller meant when he uttered the words. The full quotation is this:

God gave me my money. I believe the power to make money
is a gift from God . . . to be developed and used to the best of
our ability for the good of mankind. Having been endowed
with the gift I possess, I believe it is my duty to make money
and still more money and to use the money I make for the
good of my fellow man according to the dictates of my
conscience.[1]

Rockefeller believed that God made him rich so that he
could be a steward of God's blessings on earth—indeed, he believed the money he earned was not his but God's. Accordingly,
he believed that if he failed to give charitably, or gave unwisely,
God would withdraw His generosity.[2]

Rockefeller's ideas about charity, prosperity, and their relationship to one another were established early in his life. When
he was ten, he made a loan of $50 at 7 percent interest to a
neighbor; he was amazed when he was repaid $53.50 at the end
of the year. The concept of interest was nothing short of a miracle for him: "From that time onward I determined to make
money work for me," he said years later. He invested for the rest
of his life, his adroit use of capital making him one of the world's
richest men.[3]

Rockefeller's charitable giving had the same investment qual-
ities as his business decisions, and he evidently saw their returns
in much the same way as well. He was as assiduous a tither as he
was an investor. His personal ledger shows that, by the age of sixteen—before he had a substantial income—he was giving consistently and in a thoughtful way to a wide array of charities and
causes. He was also a talented and enthusiastic fund-raiser.
When he was twenty-one he set out to save his church from evic-
tion by its landlord by leveraging his own gifts with those of oth-

ers. He successfully raised $2,000 (about $45,000 in today's dollars), and the church was saved.

Later, as his wealth exploded after founding the Standard Oil Company, Rockefeller faced a dilemma: He wanted to continue to give, but was afraid that he could not donate enough money and still pay sufficient attention to the details of responsible philanthropy. He resolved the problem by hiring Frederick T. Gates, the man who created what Rockefeller called "scientific philanthropy," which sought to focus charitable giving in ways that would have the greatest impact and create the most beneficial opportunities for others—it amounted to a kind of venture capital for social good. The founding of the University of Chicago is an example of Rockefeller's scientific philanthropy. Rockefeller believed that this kind of giving was the most responsible way to steward "God's money" for the greatest good of mankind. And giving in this way would bring a continued flow of wealth to the giver.

Rockefeller's blending of theology and capitalism may sound odd to some. But for most Americans, who are comfortable with God *and* money, it represents an intriguing hypothesis: Charity and prosperity are interconnected. Without prosperity, large-scale charity is impossible. And without consistent and responsible charity, prosperity will not continue. According to the Rockefeller Hypothesis, giving and receiving exist in a virtuous cycle.

The Rockefeller Hypothesis is neatly summarized in John Bunyan's *Pilgrim's Progress* when the character Old Honest poses this riddle to the innkeeper Gaius:

> *A man there was, tho' some did count him mad*
> *the more he cast away, the more he had.*

Gaius interprets the verse thus:

> *He that bestows his Goods upon the Poor*
> *Shall have as much again, and ten times more.[4]*

If Gaius is right, charity is a crucial factor in the prosperity—financial and nonfinancial—of the givers themselves, not just the recipients of their charity. And this raises the stakes for all the issues in this book. If charity *causes* prosperity, selfishness causes poverty. And the forces of uncharity in America and around the world are more dangerous and corrosive than we might have thought—for nongivers, for their communities, and for entire nations.

Does the Rockefeller Hypothesis sound fanciful to you? It doesn't to many scholars, philosophers, and theologians.

Over the past decade, research on "social entrepreneurship" has shown that charitable activities create rewards of tremendous magnitude—rewards that transcend private financial returns to individuals and companies. Social entrepreneurs can be givers who donate to create high social value, which is usually not denominated in dollars. For instance, the value from an innovative program to protect poor kids from preventable diseases might be measured in the number of children vaccinated per year. Socially entrepreneurial charity may help create social and economic conditions congenial to economic development if healthier kids grow up to be productive workers. It may also bring great joy to the giver, and provide him or her a healthier community in which to live. In these ways, financial and nonfinancial benefits from charitable giving flow to the giver and spill over onto the rest of us.[5]

Charitable giving can also generate "social capital"—the trust and social cohesion a community enjoys. The most famous work on social capital comes from Robert Putnam, whose best-selling book *Bowling Alone: The Collapse and Revival of American Community* describes in great detail how social capital leads to happiness, health, and economic prosperity. Charitable acts, such as giving and volunteering, tend to strengthen social networks between people. These networks stimulate economic success, Putnam believes. He cites dozens of studies showing how networks provide employment possibilities, business opportunities, and access to financial capital. The evidence about the link between social capital and nonfinancial benefits is even more convincing. Putnam describes research showing that social networks are as important for physical health as diet, exercise, and not smoking; that socially disconnected people have shorter lives than demographically similar people who have social connections; and that the more people socialize with others the happier they are. The evidence presented in this chapter strengthens Putnam's assertion that social capital is important for the health of communities. Social capital is one more way that giving enriches givers.[6]

The social theorist George Gilder explains the correlation between charity and prosperity differently. Gilder believes that market activity is itself a sort of "charity." He argues that a good society—one in which people are generous with each other—is predicated on gifts given without guaranteed return, but made on faith in the social system. So, as is true of traditional agricultural societies, people give to each other in times of need with the expectation that the receivers will reciprocate. Gilder observes that capitalism looks remarkably like a "good society" in this way. Capitalism requires a certain amount of faith in the economic system, that it will pay positive returns. Since returns on "gifts"—investments—are not predetermined, faith becomes all the more important. In Gilder's view, charity stimulates prosperity because they both stem from the same types of motivations and actions. If this idea seems strange or extreme, consider the fact that people who invest in social enterprises tend to be commercial entrepreneurs as well—because, as Gilder would argue, the two kinds of investment are very similar.[7]

A more intuitive economic argument comes from Thorstein Veblen, the early twentieth-century economist and sociologist. Veblen believed that charity (and the related behavior of religiosity) encourages people to be industrious: "[The] residue of the religious life—the sense of communion with the environment, or with the generic life process—as well as the impulse of charity or of sociability, act in a pervasive way to shape men's habits of thought for the economic purpose." Veblen did not explain precisely why this is so, although there are some straightforward possibilities. For example, people might work harder after incurring expenditures (such as charitable gifts). Or people may work in part so that they will have money to give away. Or it may be that charity and industriousness bring each other out. Shakespeare's Pericles warned, "One sin . . . another doth provoke." Perhaps one virtue another doth provoke as well.[8]

Some social scientists believe that the link between charity and prosperity comes from the positive reaction people get when they are charitable. That is, my charity makes me better off because it makes people like me more, and they go out of their way to help me. A much subtler theory is that the benefits from charity stem from the personal transformation it provokes in the giver. According to this theory, when I give, I become more effective in all areas of my life; I am therefore happier, healthier, and more successful. Psychologists would argue that, as a giver, I am by definition a provider of help, as opposed to a victim. When I am thus empowered, my life improves in all sorts of ways.[9]

Charity can also aid a giver by providing *meaning* to that person. In his classic book *Man's Search for Meaning,* the psychiatrist Victor E. Frankl defines meaning as the objective of human striving, and he explicitly links it to charity. Frankl believes that giving can be a source of meaning, a way to personal enlightenment:

> Being human always points, and is directed, to something, or someone, other than oneself—be it a meaning to fulfill or another human being to encounter. The more one forgets himself—by giving himself to a cause to serve or another person to love—the more human he is and the more he actualizes himself . . . self-actualization is only possible as a side-effect of self-transcendence.[10]

Frankl created *logotherapy,* or "meaning-centered psychotherapy," to encourage patients to overcome psychological disorders through a focus on meaning in their lives. His concept stemmed from observations of fellow concentration camp inmates when he was a prisoner at Auschwitz. He noticed that prisoners who survived tended to have a purpose that they considered greater than themselves—something that motivated their will to survive. After the war, he found the same was true of his psychiatry patients: Once they dedicated themselves to a cause, a deed, or other people, they experienced higher personal effectiveness and functionality. In other words, charity makes people more effective and better able to prosper in all sorts of ways.

Together, the theories here suggest a comprehensive and compelling argument that charity should have positive effects on financial prosperity, national income, health, and happiness: Charitable giving is extremely pleasurable. It not only gives people the power to help others but also makes their lives meaningful. It also gives them the expressive power to support causes they care about—power the political system cannot provide—and ties them to others who have similar interests and passions. Unlike taxation and redistribution, charity is a personal choice and a voluntary sacrifice, and thus highly empowering. For all of these reasons, givers are happier than they would be if they didn't give, and probably healthier and richer. Donating money gives people one more reason to earn money, so givers naturally work harder and earn more than nongivers. It makes sense that charity should increase our happiness, health, financial well-being, and even—if enough of us give—our nation's GDP.

I have only focused here on the various ways that social scientists have explained a possible causal relationship between charity and prosperity. I have neglected what many would probably think of as the most obvious explanations of all—the religious ones. Every religious tradition makes essentially this claim. The book of Proverbs puts it this way: "One man gives freely, yet gains even more; another withholds unduly, but comes to poverty." Lest we assume that such references are only to rewards in heaven, the English theologian Matthew Henry leaves little room for doubt. For example, he interprets this Proverb as "[God] blesses the giving hand, and so makes it a getting hand." This is not limited to Western religions, either; as the Tibetan Buddhist Dalai Lama explains, "I feel from my own experience that when I practice compassion, there is an immediate direct benefit to myself . . . I get 100 percent benefit, while the benefit to others may be 50 percent."[11]

Besides receiving God's active benevolence, religious believers might derive worldly blessings—particularly happiness—from their own charity if they consciously or unconsciously view giving as an investment in their immortal souls (or karma, or future lives). There might also be great intrinsic pleasure for many people in doing what they believe God wishes for them.

Both social science theories and theology make it possible to believe that charity stimulates prosperity. But in this book, theory isn't good enough—we need data to show that charity isn't just *associated* with financial and nonfinancial prosperity but that it *causes* these things. Such data are available, and they tell us that the Rockefeller Hypothesis is right.

Let's begin with money. There is no doubt that prosperity and charity are positively correlated. We know that Americans of all income classes are generous, especially the working poor. However, as one moves up in income, the dollars given and the likelihood of giving increase substantially. This is especially true as people move up from the middle class. For example, an average American family earning $100,000 or more in 2000 was 10 percentage points more likely to give to charity, and gave a larger percentage of its household income than an average lower middle-class family earning between $30,000 and $50,000. The richer family was more likely to give to both secular and religious causes. It was also more likely to volunteer and to give in other nonfinancial ways.

The positive association between charity and income persists even when we control for other forces that might affect the relationship. For example, imagine two people who are identical with respect education, age, religion, politics, sex, and race. The only difference is that one person gives money and volunteers his or her time annually, but the other does neither. The data tell us that the charitable person will earn, on average, about $14,000 more per year than the uncharitable person.[12]

So the association between charity and prosperity is clear. The challenge is in measuring *causality:* If prosperity and charity rise and fall together, how can we tell which is pushing and which is being pushed? Although the Rockefeller Hypothesis holds that charity leads to prosperity, some conventional wisdom holds that income always comes first—you have to have something before you can give it away. On the other hand, perhaps both are right, and they affect each other. Or maybe they are not really related, and some outside force such as education is pushing giving and income in the same direction. How do we figure this out?

At the level of an individual giver, the challenge for finding a truly causal link from charity to income—if this link exists—is to isolate the part of charitable giving not caused by one's income and then look at how that part pushes income. The details of the statistical method for doing so are left for the appendix, but they work more or less as follows. Imagine I have two phenomena, X and Y, and they are related to each other. I want to know the part of the association between the two that runs only from X to Y— not vice versa. Say I can find a force Z that is a good predictor of X, but isn't related to Y. I use Z to make a prediction of the value of X—call it $\hat{X}$. If I find that $\hat{X}$ is related to Y, it can't be because Y is pushing—it is the pure effect of X on Y. For us, X is money giving and Y is income. Z is volunteering, which we have found is related to money giving but not directly to income.

Testing the relationship in this way, we find that charity pushes up income—but income increases charity as well. Money giving and prosperity exist in positive feedback to each other—a virtuous cycle, you might say. For example, in 2000, controlling for education, age, race, and all the other outside explanations for giving and income increases, a dollar donated to charity was associated with $4.35 in extra income. Of this extra income, $3.75 was due to the dollar given to charity. At the same time, each extra dollar in income stimulated 14 cents in new giving. All told, this is evidence that charity has an excellent return on investment, far better than the return from the vast majority of stocks and bonds.[13]

This finding helps explain the mystery of why low-income working people who are exceptionally generous also tend to have high levels of income mobility. These people give away a much higher portion of their money than nonworking people with equivalent total incomes. This may be part of the reason why—along with forces such as good work habits and an orientation toward opportunity instead of dependence on government aid—they are far more likely than the nonworking poor to escape from poverty in relatively short order.

At the upper end of the income scale, where charity is common, giving might be understood as an effective investment secret. The lesson for the rest of us might be that giving is important to a balanced investment strategy.

The financial advantages of giving do not stop with the individual giver—evidence shows that donations push up income even more at the level of the whole economy. We can demonstrate this by looking at average household charity and GDP per capita as they change over time. Charity and GDP levels have moved together over the years: Correcting for inflation and population changes, GDP per person in America has risen over the past fifty years by about 150 percent; charitable giving per person has risen by about 190 percent. These trends by themselves don't tell us which force is pushing and which is pulling, however. To figure that out, we need to see whether the past values of one force affect future values of the other. For instance, if an increase in last year's charity levels predict a jump in this year's GDP, the relationship can be one way only: from charity to GDP.

Once again, what we find is evidence that GDP and giving are mutually reinforcing: Economic growth pushes up charitable giving, and charitable giving pushes up economic growth. For example, in 2004, $100 in extra income per American drove about $1.47 in charitable giving per person. At the same time, a dollar in charitable giving stimulated more than $19 in income. At the national level, a 1 percent increase in national giving—about $1.9 billion in 2004—appeared to increase real GDP by about $36 billion.[14]

Let's compare the impact of charity on income for individuals, and for the nation. When someone gives a dollar to charity, a nice return goes to the giver; but the greater part of the increases in income accrue to the nation as a whole. Charity has tremendous "spillover effects," like other beneficial public services such as education, and social virtues, such as honesty. To make this point most vividly, let's imagine what would happen if private individual charitable donations in America were cut in half. This would mean about $95 billion fewer dollars each year to charities, churches, and other causes—meaning that many critical services in social welfare, health, education, the arts, religious faith, and the environment would disappear and needs would go unmet. Even more, however, we could expect about $1.8 trillion in national income to disappear as well—about 15 percent of American GDP.

Were it not for charity, America would be a significantly poorer nation than it is today. This would affect the rich and poor alike, as well as tax revenues and government-supported public services. When Ralph Nader contends that "a society that has more justice is a society that needs less charity," he has no idea of the hardship he is advocating for America's most vulnerable citizens, and for the rest of us as well.

There is a lesson here for other nations, too. It is true that factors besides charity can stimulate or depress economic growth: A culture of hard work is a particularly obvious example, and explains why Japan—where people are half as likely to volunteer as Americans, and families give less than one fifth as much to charity as American families—has been prosperous. Similarly, it stands to reason that disappointing growth in France has at least as much to do with the French population's tenuous relationship with employment (with its short work weeks, long vacations, and early retirements) as it does to low French charity. Still, charity is *one more* force helping or hurting a country's economic prosperity and, as such, should be on the radar of macroeconomists and policymakers.[15]

The link between charity and growth may also serve as a warning for American communities that are reliant on government income transfers—communities apparently resistant to economic progress. The political philosopher Irving Kristol once asserted, "The problem with our current welfare programs is not that they are costly—which they are—but that they have such perverse consequences for people they are supposed to benefit." Welfare itself—through the uncharitable behavior it tends to provoke—might thus be implicated in aggravating the social and economic conditions that lead people to need support in the first place.[16]

We already know that opportunity and charity (not equality and charity) are parallel virtues insofar as people who embrace economic freedom tend to be the most charitable. Here we see one possible explanation for why this is so. Since there is a natural symbiosis between charity and success, it is hardly surprising that charitable people seek opportunity, not forced equality. These people find themselves in a virtuous cycle of giving and receiving.

Prosperity is not simply financial; after all, we are taught practically from birth that "money can't buy happiness," and most people would surely agree that one's happiness and health are more important than money for a "prosperous" life. What is the evidence on the connection between charity, happiness, and health?[17]

Although most of the data do not establish cause-and-effect, the evidence shows that giving—especially giving in ways other than money—goes along with happiness and health. One survey of Americans shows that people who give money charitably are 43 percent more likely to say they are "very happy" than nongivers; nongivers are three and a half times more likely than givers to say they are "not happy at all." (In this way, it appears that money *can* buy happiness—via one's favorite charity.) Similarly, volunteers are 42 percent more likely than nonvolunteers to say they are very happy. The patterns are the same for good health. Givers are 25 percent more likely than nongivers to say their health is excellent or very good; nongivers about twice as likely as givers to say their health is poor or fair.[18]

Generous people are not happy and healthy just because of other forces such as income and education, which might also stimulate charitable behavior—the connection with generosity is genuine. Consider two people who are identical with respect to religion, age, income, education, gender, number of children, marital status, and race, but one volunteers at least once each year and the other does not. On average, the volunteer will enjoy greater happiness and better health than the nonvolunteer. Specifically, the volunteer is 9 percentage points more likely to say that he or she is "very happy" than the identical nonvolunteer, and 4 points more likely to say that his or her health is "excellent."[19]

Happiness and health benefits are apparent in other types of charity as well. For example, consider the 15 percent of Americans who donate blood at least once a year. These people are 27 percent more likely than nondonors to say they are very happy. They are also 33 percent more likely than nondonors to say they enjoy excellent health. These numbers alone are not evidence that giving blood makes a person healthy and happy because unhealthy people will not give blood, and they will also be unhappy because of their poor health. Therefore, let us look only at people who say their health is excellent (about a third of the population). Imagine two people in excellent health who are identical with respect to income, education, age, sex, race, religion, and political views, but one gives blood and the other does not. The donor will be 9 percentage points more likely to say that he or she is very happy than the nondonor.[20]

Many studies come to similar conclusions about the association between charity and good health. Some studies even establish a strong connection between voluntarism and the length of one's life. Several large studies of the elderly, for example, show that senior citizens who volunteer enjoy a 40 percent lower probability of dying in a given year than people of the same age and health level. Furthermore, researchers have commonly found that—no surprise at this point—the benefits are greatest among people who also participate in religious activities.[21]

Still, this evidence tells us only that charity, happiness, and good health are associated with each other. Can we establish causality? This might seem even harder than for money prosperity because happiness and health are highly subjective and therefore messier to measure. Perhaps it will come as a surprise to some, then, that psychologists have used experiments—similar to drug tests—to establish that giving behavior does indeed cause us to be healthier and happier.

In one famous study, researchers at Harvard Medical School conducted an experiment in which a group of 132 multiple sclerosis patients was split into two groups; one group was assigned to act charitably toward members of the other. The researchers found that the givers experienced a "dramatic change in their lives": In confidence, self-awareness, and depression, they enjoyed between three and seven times more improvement than the receivers of help. The researchers recommended that helping others should be incorporated more routinely into therapy for patients recovering from illnesses.[22]

In another study using a sample of American Presbyterians, researchers at the University of Massachusetts Medical School found that formal volunteering caused significant improvements to mental health, and that givers were significantly more likely to benefit than the receivers of help. (They also found that major predictors of being a helper included prayer activities and high church involvement.) In an interview about the research, the lead author of the Presbyterians' study explained the findings by saying that "when you open your heart to other people to listen and care about them, it changes the way you look at the world and you're happier." Similar studies have shown that directly after donating their time, volunteers have experienced depression relief, weight control, immune system improvements, chronic pain reduction, lower blood pressure, and reduced symptoms of indigestion, asthma, and arthritis. Furthermore, studies have found that the more one volunteers, the greater the benefits.[23]

In summary, happiness, health, and income coexist in a self-reinforcing cycle with charity: Happy, healthy, successful, opportunity-oriented people are most likely to give and to volunteer. At the same time, charitable people are more likely than uncharitable people to be happy, healthy, and financially prosperous. Yes, prosperous people are more likely to give to charity—but charity can also make them prosperous and more likely to make even more charitable contributions.

Charity appears to help us financially and to improve our health and happiness. But evidence suggests that charity is also a crucial element in our ability to govern ourselves as a free people.

In *Democracy in America,* Alexis de Tocqueville asserted that "civil associations pave the way for political ones." Tocqueville believed that American democracy depended on an involved citizenry that not only made its wishes known to elected officials but also held politicians accountable to voters. Active citizenship was, in turn, a function of participation in community organizations, charities, and other causes that were neither government-created nor work-related but based on mutual trust, a sense of equality, and interreliance between citizens.[24]

In their seminal 1977 book *To Empower People: From State to Civil Society,* the economist Peter L. Berger and the theologian Richard John Neuhaus applied Tocqueville's assertion to America in the late twentieth century. They contended that people, not governments, were best positioned to make critical decisions of social importance, and that "mediating structures" between the state and its citizens that empowered them to do so should be protected and incorporated into policymaking. What were these mediating structures? Neighborhoods, churches, families, and voluntary associations. The stakes, as they saw them, were too high to ignore. They warned that, unless America changed course soon, governments would take over the traditional role of churches in American society: "The danger today is not that churches or any one church will take over the state. The much more real danger is that the state will take over the functions of the church."[25]

Berger and Neuhaus did not advocate a destruction of the government, nor did they launch an antigovernment crusade. On the contrary, they simply promised a freer, more democratic society if government would just work together with mediating structures, instead of against them.

In 1977, these ideas seemed tremendously radical because at that time American public policy was moving away from reliance on the private sector and toward a continual expansion of the welfare state. Jimmy Carter, the last of the "big-government presidents," was in the White House. The so-called Christian Right had not yet fully emerged as a coherent political force to advocate for the rights of churches and communities. Public school students (myself included) were being forcibly bused out of their neighborhoods to comply with racial mixing criteria set by bureaucrats and judges.

What a contrast with America today. The changes in political currents over the past thirty years are a subject for other authors, but Berger and Neuhaus's proposition has been embraced by the moderate left and the moderate right, and their once-radical ideas are now "mainstream." Most policymakers now advocate the use of "faith-based organizations" in the distribution of social services. Most students are once again in their neighborhood schools. And politicians extol the virtues of faith and family. In short, it is now accepted that neighborhoods, churches, families, and voluntary associations are important to the effective functioning of our democracy.[26]

How are Berger and Neuhaus's mediating structures supported? In no small part, through charity. Private gifts of money and time provide the primary support for American churches, community organizations, and many nonprofits. If we accept Berger and Neuhaus's argument—which more and more Americans do—we must conclude that private giving is essential to the protection of our free society and the exercise of our democratic values.

Plenty of empirical evidence adds support to this claim: People who give are far more likely to be active political participants than people who do not give. In 2000, people who gave money or volunteered were more than twice as likely as those who did not to attend a political meeting that year, participate in a political group, or belong to a group taking local action for political reform. In 2004, people who belonged to voluntary associations were 16 percentage points more likely to say they followed public affairs than those who did not belong to voluntary groups, 25 points more likely to vote in almost every election if they were eligible, and 26 points more likely to contact their elected officials in a given year.[27]

Real-life cases provide even more evidence of how giving can enhance citizenship. As an example, take the neighborhood of Red Hook, in Brooklyn, New York. This neighborhood was one of the poorest, most drug-infested, crime-filled neighborhoods in New York City in the mid-1990s. One catalytic event—the murder of a popular school principal—mobilized community activists, city leaders, and policymakers to change Red Hook with the aid of a large volunteer force. The effect was a dramatic economic and social transformation of the neighborhood. Volunteer groups patrolled the neighborhood, cleaned up streets, and organized meetings to improve the relationship between police and residents. Residents became involved as volunteers.[28]

On the morning of September 11, 2001, Red Hook—directly across the East River from the World Trade Center—was deeply affected by the terrorist attack on the twin towers: Red Hook's two fire companies lost twelve firefighters. In response to the tragedy, the residents volunteered to provide provisions to rescue crews and survivors of the attack—unthinkable only a few years before. Their voluntarism gave them the opportunity to express themselves fully as good citizens.[29]

⌐◯

In the first half of this book, we looked carefully at the trends and pressures in modern life that depress our charitable impulses. Secularism, forced income redistribution, welfare, and family breakdown are all phenomena implicated in depressing the levels of money charity, volunteering, and informal acts of generosity. As we have always known, a consequence of low charity is less support for important causes: Fewer resources are available to aid the poor; houses of worship are less able to reach out to new people; community groups are less successful at mobilizing neighbors for mutual benefit; people receive fewer acts of kindness in their daily lives. Undoubtedly, our society is impoverished when charity is depressed.

But the evidence in this chapter ups the ante. The data on giving and volunteering tell us that charity is an important element in the prosperity, health, and happiness of givers themselves, not just the recipients of their charity. It also contributes to the economic prosperity and democratic freedoms we enjoy as a nation in the United States—and there is no reason to suspect this is untrue in other countries. Indeed, the anemic economic growth rates of most Western European countries may be partially explained by Europeans' low rates of charitable behavior.

For some, even in spite of the theory and evidence, the argument that charity stimulates prosperity, happiness, health, and good citizenship may still be counterintuitive. We can certainly use more research from all disciplines into the charity-prosperity relationship. But the evidence here suggests that the burden of proof lies with anyone who would claim that giving does *not* stimulate prosperity. Until we have decisive evidence that this is *not* so, we should as individuals and as a country assume—and act on the assumption—that just as American charity relies on our overall prosperity, so, too, does our prosperity rely on a willingness to give. And just as charity is an excellent investment for individuals, so it is for our communities and our nation.

If charity is so important, can't we just guarantee the economic and social benefits by taxing people and using the revenues for important social projects? By no means. This would have just the opposite effect. As we all know (and have experienced), forced "giving" through taxation lowers work incentives—if you can't keep the money you earn, you tend to work less. This explains why governments can and often do experience falling tax revenues when they raise tax rates. Government income redistribution thus not only lowers working individuals' incomes but also inhibits economic growth. This is not a matter of political opinion; we know this to be true, consider it a cost of public policy, and try to balance the tradeoff between personal prosperity and income equality. Even liberal economists recognize this tradeoff. Arthur Okun, the chairman of President Lyndon B. Johnson's Council of Economic Advisors, wrote: "The money must be carried from the rich to the poor in a leaky bucket. Some of it will simply disappear in transit, so the poor will not receive all the money that is taken from the rich." Okun was referring not just to the bureaucratic waste in the government; he also knew that redistribution lowered incentives to earn money.[30]

But private charity is a bucket with no leaks, and without tradeoffs. When we give freely, we are richer, and the people and causes we give to are better off, too. This is why redistributive policies that lower private giving incentives, and political ideologies that substitute the state for private action, are so dangerous—they squander the magical synergy between generosity and productivity. Some people will always say that government spending (based on taxes) is necessary to pay for things that private charity will not. This may be true. But we must remember that taxation has some destructive consequences for communities and for the nation as a whole. Charity, by contrast, has only the upside.

Many political conservatives see—in the policies of the political left—symptoms of a deep cultural malaise. One symptom, we often hear, is secularism, which exemplifies the lack of transcendental meaning in modern society. Others cite the support for high government income redistribution levels, which (some say) comes from a weak work ethic and a declining spirit of self-reliance. But might it be that forces such as secularism and redistribution are not just symptoms but also *causes* of a cultural problem? These forces exert downward pressure on voluntary charity, as we know. And lower charity leads to less happiness, worse health, and probably greater poverty. A good way to help break a cycle of cultural malaise might be to confront the effects of secularism and overweening governments and to encourage more giving.

Political conservatives are not the only ones, however, who argue that the conditions of modern life have created a malaise. Political liberals point to the raw market forces that increasingly govern our day-to-day lives and, they believe, encourage selfishness by rewarding dog-eat-dog behavior. One popular book argues that rampant capitalism lurks behind an epidemic of selfish, unethical acts by Americans who are simply trying to "get ahead." This capitalism is exemplified by the corporate scandals of the past several years—such as the collapse of the Enron Corporation—but, some argue, it pervades our everyday lives in smaller ways as well. For example, many in academia believe that academic cheating by students is on the rise because of the perceived job market pressures to excel at the university. A softer, less market-oriented culture might create incentives to be honest and charitable with one another—leading, perhaps, to a virtuous cycle with happiness and prosperity.[31]

Unfortunately, the two sides of this debate—although probably in agreement that there is a pall over much of American culture—propose solutions that are incompatible. The right suggests that we need more freedom—especially economic freedom—for our families and communities to prosper, and less government intrusion. The left generally advocates more government in economic life to lower the rewards to "cutthroat capitalism," equalize resources across the population, and provide more public goods and services. Some liberal economists suggest that the solution to our cultural ills lies in taxing our incomes at much higher rates specifically to curtail useless consumer spending. For conservatives, new policies to tax and redistribute income would thrust us ever deeper into the malaise from which we already suffer. This book does not completely settle these competing arguments. However, we can say that charity is a potent solution to the cultural problems identified by both sides. And charity is *not* aided by expanding the government's role in economic life, by and large.[32]

What are the "right" public policies to encourage lots of giving? Even more important, what are the right attitudes and behaviors for our families and communities? At this point in the book, you probably have your own answers to this question. The last chapter gives mine.

CHAPTER 8

THE WAY FORWARD

Every man must decide whether he will walk in the creative light of altruism or the darkness of destructive selfishness. This is the judgment. Life's persistent and most urgent question is "What are you doing for others?"

DR. MARTIN LUTHER KING JR.

There is a story about W. C. Fields on his deathbed. Outside his hospitable room, Fields heard a poor newsboy in the snow wailing, "Wuxtry! Wuxtry! Stock Market Prices Fall!" Moved with compassion, he remarked to those gathered around him, "Poor little urchins out there—undernourished, no doubt improperly clad—something's got to be done about them, something's got to be done." After reflecting for a few moments, however, he concluded, "On second thought, screw 'em."[1]

W. C. Fields obviously doesn't speak for Charitable America. But does he speak for Selfish America?

I don't think so. I don't believe that most of the Americans who never give or volunteer are walking around thinking, "Screw 'em" about the less fortunate. Rather, they are unaware, caught in a series of political and cultural institutions that makes giving harder than it should be, and harboring the dangerous misconception that they are charitable—when they are not. Further, they do not know why private charity is so critically important for their success and America's—and why private charity has no substitutes.

So the question for this concluding chapter is this: What must we do to shrink Selfish America and grow Charitable America?

Let's start with one of the big themes in this book: government. We have seen again and again how it can function to suppress charity. The government's ability to redistribute income to increase economic equality, as useful and important as some people think this is, displaces the private responsibility some people feel to give voluntarily. Welfare payments suppress giving tendencies. And subsidies to nonprofit organizations "crowd out" private giving by changing the incentives of givers.

The government is not entirely to blame for any of these effects. We are free people in America, and responsible for our own decisions to give, or not. "Crowding out" is hardly an excuse for personal selfishness. Still, governments may destroy value in wholly misunderstood ways if private charity falls when they subsidize nonprofit organizations or redistribute income. A balance must be struck between our need to pay for some services through tax revenues and the ill-effects that come from lower private charity. At the very least, policymakers need to recognize that some policies lower private giving and so impose costs on our communities and nation.

Sometimes the government discourages charities in more direct ways than just crowding out, though. Government regulations often make it difficult or impossible to engage in charitable activities in the first place. The American nonprofit sector is filled with stories of the government roadblocks to charitable and civic activities—such as onerous legal requirements, punitive mandatory expenditures, and impossible hiring practices. The manager of one private drug rehabilitation clinic in San Francisco, for instance, complained that her agency "had to fight every bureaucracy that exists." Relying on volunteers to help clients instead of state-certified teachers, drug counselors, and social workers, the agency quickly ran afoul of government requirements. In the manager's colorful words: "If Jesus Christ walked in today and wanted to start Christianity, he wouldn't be able to do it because [the government would] say to him, 'You need two psychiatrists, you need one social worker, somebody has to sign the things.'"[2]

Similar stories are part of life for average people who never run a charitable organization. Here is my own real-life example. In 2004, my wife and I adopted a little girl from a Chinese orphanage. Anyone who has dealt with the Chinese government might expect a complicated bureaucratic process on that side of the adoption. What truly took us aback, however, was the awful red tape imposed by various levels of government in the United States. The worst of the process involved New York State—notorious for its punishing taxation and torturous regulatory environment—which made every step in the process of gathering dozens of adoption documents painful and expensive. For example, the

Chinese government required an affidavit showing that my wife and I had no criminal past. This was available from the local police department, but the document had to be authenticated by a New York State authority. The affidavit had to be notarized by a licensed notary in our county of residence. The notary's stamp had to be certified by the county clerk, and the county clerk's stamp had to be certified by New York's secretary of state. Document preparation in a New York adoption takes at least six months of notarizing, certifying, authenticating, renotarizing. During this time, our daughter sat in an orphanage. I have talked to dozens of people who claim they would adopt a child if the process weren't so difficult and expensive. Is it hyperbole to say that the price of bureaucracy includes the lives of these un-adopted children? Readers can decide for themselves.

Perhaps adoption seems like a special case. Let's look at something more common: Say you live in New Jersey and want to help out with your child's Little League team. Simple, right? Not so fast. First, you'll need to comply with New Jersey's "Minimum Standards for Volunteer Coaches' Safety Orientation and Training Skills Programs" to protect yourself from being sued. To wit:

(a) The minimum standards set forth in this subchapter identify the major topics which must be addressed in volunteer coaching/managing/officiating programs for safety orientation and training skills programs required for civil immunity according to N.J.S.A. 2A:62 6 et seq. The topics must be presented within the context of an educational program that addresses the perspective of the specific population(s) of athletes served (for example, young, senior, disabled, novice and skilled athletes).

(b) In order to be covered by the provisions for civil immunity as prescribed by New Jersey P.L. 1988, c. 87 (N.J.S.A. 2A:62A 6 et seq.), the volunteer athletic coach, manager or official must attend a safety orientation and skills training program of at least a three hour duration which meets the minimum standards set forth in this subchapter. The programs may be provided by local recreation departments, non profit organizations and national/state sports training organizations. The standards apply to all volunteer athletic programs in New Jersey regardless of population served.

(c) Any organization providing a safety orientation and skills training program pursuant to these rules, shall issue a certificate of participation to each participant who successfully completes [the en]tire program.[3]

And so on. Maybe volunteering wasn't such a good idea after all.

Alright then. Why not make a contribution to your child's public school? In some places, governments have decreed that this would not be fair to the schools you *didn't* give to. In Portland, Oregon, your child's school can keep the first $5,000 in donations it receives each year, but the school district taxes away a third of anything beyond that. It costs you $1.50 to give your child's school $1—essentially a negative tax deduction. In the mind of Portland's policymakers, resources to schools are less important than school equality. Once again, we see that it is freedom and opportunity—not equality—that are charity's sister virtues.[4]

It seems ridiculously obvious that the government should not suppress charity through bureaucratic rules and procedures. Yet this occurs with depressing regularity. Agenda item number one for policymakers should be to make sure this doesn't happen.

The government shouldn't suppress charity, but should it take active measures to stimulate it? Maybe even mandate it by law? Policymakers have tried to do just this. For example, the State of Rhode Island has set in its statutes that people *must* be Good Samaritans, under penalty of law: "Any person at the scene of an emergency who knows that another person is exposed to or has suffered grave physical harm shall . . . give reasonable assistance to the exposed person." Similar statutes exist in Minnesota, Wisconsin, and Vermont.[5]

Many recent initiatives have ordered voluntarism in the public schools. The former governor of New Jersey proposed that an alternative to some coursework requirements for graduation from the state's high schools be "volunteering in an approved community program." Bringing new meaning to "volunteering," many school districts require that students perform a minimum number of hours of community service before they are awarded diplomas.[6]

These kinds of laws and policies—particularly the Good Samaritan type laws—seem sensible to me. What is not clear is whether they can create anything like the benefits—financial and nonfinancial—that accrue from voluntary charity. I suspect not. An Eastern European colleague once gave me an interesting example of why this might be so: In Soviet times, some Eastern European nations mandated a certain amount of "volunteering" by citizens to the state—to clean up parks, maintain public spaces, and so forth. Voluntarism in these countries became a much despised symbol of state oppression. I am confident that American programs to encourage or mandate voluntarism would not have such extreme effects, but the lesson is worth considering nonetheless.

Some have suggested that good old-fashioned shaming is another way the government could, and sometimes does, encourage charitable giving. For example, the year after publicly released tax records showed that Al Gore, the former vice president, gave only 0.2 percent of his family income to charity (one tenth the national average), he publicly increased his giving to 6.8 percent. Some have suggested that the Internal Revenue Service should use this principle among the general population by creating a public "donation registry" that lists the percentage of income people give to charity. Although inclusion on the list would be voluntary, there would be great social pressure for some people (for example, public figures) to list themselves—and thus give more than they otherwise would, to avoid embarrassment.[7]

This approach is intriguing, but it is also problematic. It injects governments deeply into intensely private decisions—with unknown effects on charity's benefits to givers themselves. Resentfully giving out of an effort to avoid shame hardly seems conducive to the transformative effects that would help make you healthy, happy, and rich. Furthermore, if such a system revealed the causes people gave to, there is no doubt that it would change giving patterns. It might be good for unobjectionable charities such as the United Way, but it would probably hurt groups involved with controversial causes, such as those on both sides of the abortion debate. And this would weaken charity as a unique form of expression.

Financial incentives are another means by which the government can and does try to encourage charitable behavior. At the federal level in the United States and other countries, as well as in many states and municipalities, qualified nonprofit organizations are exempt from paying corporate taxes. This benefit comes in return for not distributing profits to corporate owners and so reduces the incentive to maximize profits at the public's expense. This tax exemption represents a large subsidy from government to the charitable sector; for example, a for-profit hospital pays corporate taxes on its earnings, but a Catholic hospital does not.[8]

But an even bigger subsidy comes in the form of tax revenues lost on tax-deductible contributions to charity. The federal government and most states allow donors to qualified charities and causes to deduct their contributions from their taxable income, the idea being to give people tax incentives to donate. This constitutes a huge government "matching grant" program. If I make a charitable contribution and itemize my deductions when I prepare my tax return, I can deduct the amount I donate from my taxable income. Thus, if I contribute $100 and my tax rate is 36 percent, the government is effectively matching a $64 gift of mine with $36 in lost tax revenues. The total amount of these "indirect subsidies" from tax-deductible donations runs into the billions. The Internal Revenue Service, for example, estimates that in 2002, individuals donated and deducted more than $140 billion in money and in-kind gifts (this is less than total private giving, much of which is not deducted for tax purposes). This figure represents foregone income tax revenues—and hence the government indirect subsidy—of about $40 billion per year from the federal government and a substantial amount from states and municipalities.[9]

The tax deduction for donations does create an incentive to give and is therefore an example of how governments *can* stimulate charitable behavior. Unfortunately, this incentive is not available to everybody. Most low-income families do not receive this benefit because they cannot afford enough deductible expenses—

including donations—to make tax itemization worthwhile. Although nearly eight households in ten in the top 20 percent of the income distribution itemize their tax deductions each year, only two in ten in the bottom 20 percent do so. And even if a low-income family itemizes to get a deduction on its contributions, the progressive structure of the U.S. tax system makes the matching portion from the government less generous for them than it is for the rich because they face a much lower tax rate. For example, if my tax rate is 15 percent, the government covers a smaller portion of my contribution than if my tax rate is 35 percent. Not surprisingly, tax incentives to give charitably create disproportionate benefits for the nonprofits supported by rich people, such as elite health organizations, private universities, and arts groups. Meanwhile, organizations supported by the poor—religious organizations in particular—tend to receive far less indirect government support. Indeed, if donors to churches (49 percent of whom itemize their deductions) had the same tax incentives as donors to private universities (63 percent of whom itemize), a small increase in tax incentives would release billions of dollars in gifts to houses of worship and other faith-based nonprofits.[10]

The government needs to address this bias against the poor—and their favored charities. Possible solutions might include allowing deductions for giving even if a person does not itemize, or creating a system in which the tax deduction is not dependent on an individual's income level. A tax credit for giving that is the same for everyone would do the trick, as would a "flat" income tax. Another idea is to offer people the option either of paying a certain amount in taxes or of receiving a tax credit for the equivalent amount given to a recognized charity. For example, say you earn $25,000 and the federal government implements a "tax-or-give" policy at the level of a flat 1 percent. Your choice would be to pay $250 in taxes or to give $250 to charity instead.[11]

My research on the economics of charity over the years has focused a lot on public policy and government giving incentives, and this section has given only a taste of all of the issues involved. Here is my overall assessment on the topic: Government at its best does a modest amount of good for charity with incentives to give. Policies such as tax-deductibility for contributions are sensible, but they will never create a population of givers. On the other hand, government at its worst can create massive damage by putting barriers in the way of giving.

—

What can we do personally to promote charity? The ridiculously simple answer is to give more—more money, more time, more of everything. A harder question is how to elicit giving in others.

Let's start with the people closest to us. We know plenty of ways to teach charity within our families, and I have discussed many of them in this book. First, giving charitably oneself provides a model to follow—one that children (and probably others) do indeed emulate. Second, children are more likely to learn charity in a religious environment. The effect of religion on children's giving persists after they grow up and move away, even if they don't practice their faith. Third, children brought up to believe that it is the "government's responsibility" to resolve all issues of need for themselves and others are less likely to be personally charitable than children taught that aiding others is their personal responsibility. Fourth, government assistance programs have a damaging impact on private giving, which may even provoke a cycle of dependence and hamper economic mobility. Fifth, a strong family life is an important part of the best environment to teach charitable giving.

We have a great deal of control over the lives of our children—but what about people outside our own home? Is there a way to teach charity more broadly? This is a complicated question, but there are some interesting examples of what such initiatives might look like.

The nonprofit organization Common Cents in New York City is one success story. This organization is "dedicated to advancing social justice and equal opportunity by emboldening a generation of young people to become community activists and good citizens during their youth." Despite a mission that makes it sound as if the organization were training children to agitate for government income redistribution, the organization's primary focus is on giving young kids in New York City a chance to experience philanthropy from the angle of the giver.[12]

Common Cents challenges students in New York's public schools to collect pennies from family, friends, and neighbors. Classes of students are given the "25 Sack Challenge," in which the children fill twenty-five canvas bags with pennies (about $1,000). After achieving this goal, the students collaboratively decide on worthy charitable causes in their communities. In the process, they learn a great deal about the needs of their communities. According to Adam Seidel, Common Cents' program manager, it is the personal experience of giving that has the real impact on students. He says that through the giving act—which includes meeting the recipients of gifts—children realize their "interconnectedness" with their community. And there is evidence that the organization's programs are successful in making children permanently more charitable. For example, teachers in classrooms participating in the program have reported that 96 percent of students involved in the collection and disbursement of money had an increased awareness of community needs, 95 percent were more aware of the value of contributing to their community than they were before, and 84 percent had a "reinforced sense of generosity." Interestingly, the program may make the organization's adult staff more personally charitable as well: According to Mr. Seidel, being around kids who are making a difference makes one ask, "What am *I* doing?" All in all, Common Cents not only provides kids and adults with the power of charity's moral choice but empowers them to create opportunities for others.[13]

Another interesting program targets adults. A number of community foundations—private organizations that pool philanthropic funds in specific communities and disperse them to meet local needs—have established programs that encourage young professionals to see philanthropic giving as important to their careers. For example, the Central New York Community Foundation's "Philanthropy, Involvement, and Empowerment Project" was established in 2004 to pool the resources of a group of fifteen young executives from commercial firms, government, and nonprofit agencies. This group established a common philanthropic fund that makes donations to local nonprofit organizations according to group consensus. The project's organizers believe that by giving these young professionals the chance to be philanthropists, charitable giving will become a habit for them.[14]

⌐○

Common Cents and the Central New York Community Foundation are unusual in that they stress the benefits of charity for donors as well as recipients. Alas, many charitable organizations do not see giving as anything more than as a means to an end. This needs to change.

Donations of time and money are essential. Money donations make up 20 percent of all the funds to America's nonprofit sector, including 16 percent ($19 billion) to educational organizations such as private universities, 20 percent ($15 billion) to social welfare nonprofits such as homeless shelters and soup kitchens, and 84 percent ($67 billion) to religious organizations—mostly houses of worship. Similarly, the value of volunteer time to educational institutions in 1998 was $23 billion; it was $21 billion for social welfare; and $31 billion for religious groups. Without private charitable gifts of time and money—not to mention the informal charity that is never summed up in official statistics—many of the services in education, arts, religion, and relief for the needy would not exist.[15]

But the value of charity is not limited to those who receive the services that giving makes possible. The evidence in this book shows that charity unleashes enormous benefits not only to the givers themselves but also to their families, communities, and the nation. Everyone understands that charitable organizations create value by providing for the needy. What many organizations misunderstand is who the "needy" truly are. In addition to those in need of food, shelter, education, the needy are also those who *need* to give to attain their full potential in happiness, health, and material prosperity—which is every one of us.

"To give away money is an easy matter and in any man's power," Aristotle said. "But to decide to whom to give it, and how large, and when, and for what purpose and how, is neither in every man's power nor an easy matter." This is a problem almost everyone faces when thinking about charity. Rockefeller solved the problem by hiring a brilliant manager to administer his "scientific philanthropy." Most of us rely on reputable charitable institutions to steward our donations properly to create the social value we seek. Charitable causes—for the most part, nonprofit organizations in the United States and Europe—therefore have a crucial role in the prosperity of our societies: They are the conduits between those who need services and those who need to give. I'll go even further: For a nonprofit organization to pass up a donation, or to neglect to raise private donations, is tantamount to leaving a person hungry.

Do most nonprofit organizations comprehend this? Apparently not. Consider the data on social welfare nonprofit organizations in the United States in 2002. Approximately 35,000 in the areas of human services—services for the poor, the disabled, and so forth—have annual revenues above $25,000. Of these organizations, 19 percent do not receive any donations. Even further, 65 percent say they do not spend any money at all to raise funds. It would be unreasonable to assert that this indicates negligence on the part of every one of the approximately 23,000 social welfare nonprofits in the United States that do not fund-raise because many probably have plausible reasons for not spending resources on fund-raising. For example, some may receive abundant donations without spending any of their resources on eliciting gifts. But surely this is not always so: Nonprofits that say they spend some amount of money on fund-raising are 25 percentage points more likely to have positive donations than those that do not. Furthermore, fund-raising organizations receive, on average, more than five times as much donated income each year as nonprofits that don't fund-raise.[16]

How do nonprofits that do not fund-raise support their organizations? Usually, their funds come from the government.

There is a clear negative correlation between government funding and private donations for most types of nonprofits. Those relying more on government money tend to receive less private charitable support than those relying less on government money. This is not surprising given that government funding "crowds out" private giving.

The best charitable organizations understand that they exist not only for their clients, but also their donors. An executive from the Latter-day Saint Foundation, an organization dedicated to providing Mormons with opportunities to give charitably, stated the foundation's mission thus: "We exist . . . to help donors change or save lives." Firms dedicated to nonprofit marketing and fund-raising are similarly aware that giving creates huge value for donors—particularly younger donors, who give to "make a difference"—and advocate donor treatment that reflects this. Merkle-Domain, a major nonprofit marketing firm in Seattle, tells its nonprofit clients that a younger donor wants to "*know* and *feel* that her giving makes a difference." Providing donors with what they need and want increases their donations—as we would expect in any situation in which someone is offered a more highly valued product. In the company's words: "[The donor] puts more demands on the organization she supports—she wants more information and involvement. When she gets what she wants from a nonprofit, she also offers more rewards: larger gifts, better retention, and more upgrade potential."[17]

Far from being a "necessary evil," fund-raising is a valuable service to a nonprofit's community in and of itself. Nonprofits should approach fund-raising with this in mind. Rather than seeing themselves as supplicants, as if donations were unilateral transfers from the giver to the organization, nonprofit executives should see the solicitation of donations as the offer of a valuable product—essential to every potential donor's happiness, health, and good fortune.

Consider this: On average, a charity embarking on a fundraising appeal can expect one person to respond per one hundred who have not given before to the charity. Among these first-time givers, the number giving a second time will be about twenty in a hundred. Of these second-time givers, fifty in a hundred will give a third time. People get hooked on their favorite charities because these charities give them what they *need*. Giving doesn't make them feel better—it makes them better. Fund-raising studies show that donors do not need mugs, T-shirts, or Bibles. Donors *do* need a good cause and prompt evidence that their donations are needed and used wisely. These are the things that help unlock charity's transformative power in givers.[18]

How can we help charitable organizations take their fund-raising more seriously? First, governments should not aid and abet the neglect of private fund-raising. Yet governments do precisely this every day. Studies show that nonprofit managers tend to fund-raise less when they receive government money. Indeed, fund-raising is frequently an impermissible use of government funds. Governments should not suffocate fund-raising efforts in this way. I am not arguing that governments stop supporting nonprofits; rather, I am suggesting that governments encourage private charity by giving preference to organizations that take fund-raising seriously. If this means that rich nonprofits get richer—because good fund-raisers get the most government money—so be it.[19]

As donors, we may also bear some responsibility for the neglect of the fund-raising by charities. When you receive a piece of mail from a charity asking for a contribution, how does the organization show you that it is efficient? Most likely, it will claim—

notwithstanding the letter in your hand—that it spends very lit-tle on fund-raising. One prominent national nonprofit rating company gives numerical scores to individual U.S. nonprofits, and the scores fall as fund-raising levels rise. Nonprofits receive the lowest possible score if their fund-raising exceeds 15 percent of revenues. This is a firm dedicated to giving people information on the quality of nonprofits and so guide giving decisions. As such, this standard instructs givers to give more to nonprofits that do not expend resources on fund-raising. This standard is mistaken. Of course, wasteful spending by a charity is unaccept-able. But an organization that spends little time or energy raising donations is forgoing revenues that it could potentially spend on its mission. Even further, it is missing the chance to help people give. It is an error to reward organizations that neglect fund-raising by giving them a donation.[20]

⌐⌐

This book has shown that one of the greatest political hypocrisies of our time is the pious sloganeering about liberals in America being more compassionate than conservatives. This stereotype is false, and it is a disservice to our country.

Let's review four major facts about charity and politics. First, there is a huge "charity gap" that follows religion: Religious peo-ple are far more charitable with their time and money than secu-larists. Religious people are more generous in informal ways as well, such as giving blood, giving money to family members, and behaving honestly. Religious people are far more likely than sec-ularists to be politically conservative. Second, people who be-lieve—as liberals often do—that the government should equalize income give and volunteer far less than people who do not believe this. Third, the American working poor are, relative to their income, very generous. The nonworking poor, however—those on public assistance—give at extremely low levels. The charitable working poor tend to be far more politically conservative than the nonworking poor. Fourth, charitable giving is learned, reinforced, and practiced within intact families—especially religious families. Secularism and family breakdown occur less frequently among conservatives than liberals. The net effect of these four facts is that conservatives generally behave more charitably than liberals, especially with respect to money donations. Much of this difference comes in gifts to religious causes, but conservatives also give and volunteer generously with secular charities.

The late Senator Daniel Patrick Moynihan once said, "The central conservative truth is that it is culture, not politics, that determines the success of a society. The central liberal truth is that politics can change a culture and save it from itself." What are the political lessons for charity? Specifically, since all of us, no matter what our political views, *should* care about personal charity, what constructive lessons are there in this information? How do we need to rethink our attitudes about giving?[21]

First of all, we should at least get our facts straight about charity. For too long, liberals have been claiming they are the most virtuous members of American society. Although they usually give less to charity, they have nevertheless lambasted conservatives for their callousness in the face of social injustice. It is a bitter irony, but one for which liberals do not bear all the blame. Conservatives have been too fixated on a kind of manly free-market rhetoric that has prevented them, by and large, from stating—or even *seeing*, the obvious fact: *Conservatives are charitable.*

Is there anything liberals can do to render legitimate their claim that they are the compassionate ones?

To begin with, the left needs to eschew its vocal radical wing that disdains charity. Ralph Nader says openly ("A society that has more justice is a society that needs less charity") what I personally have found a lot of people on the left say privately. Charitable liberals must stand up to those who would claim that voluntary gifts of money and time are to be despised rather than admired.

American liberals also need to acknowledge that they are in the minority when it comes to ideas about inequality and redistribution. The idea that income inequality is terrible per se is anachronistic and bad for charity. The evidence is clear that most Americans—including the working poor—are more interested in opportunity than in forced equality. This is a fact: There is nothing the matter with Kansas unless you are a liberal politician who is having a hard time winning votes. Income equality—when it comes at the cost of freedom and economic opportunity—is not a mainstream American value.

Income redistribution is a core liberal principle of the Democrats, which makes difficult much fundamental reconsideration of redistributive government programs. But the party can still make progress. Bill Clinton understood the behavioral implications of chronic welfare dependence, and in 1996 he took a courageous line against hard-liners in his own political party to reform the American welfare system. From the standpoint of private giving, this represents progress for the Democrats, for the poor, and for charity. Liberals can continue to build on this progress with a more realistic view of the negative social impacts of government redistribution efforts.

A major problem facing liberal charity is an often unreflective faith that government offers the best possible solution to social ills. Liberals often believe that problems such as poverty and crime are *societal,* and thus on such a scale that they can be ameliorated effectively only through government programs. Conservatives, in contrast, usually see problems in individuals and communities. I'm not adjudicating the inherent legitimacy of these viewpoints in this book, but I am pointing out that the liberal view is generally uncongenial to individual charitable action. This view discourages a personal sense that an individual's time and treasure can meaningfully help solve social problems, and it diminishes individual charity. This is not a theoretical point about the difference between liberals and conservatives. It is what the data show to be true.

Finally, a barrier to liberal giving is the rise of liberal secularism. In a fundamentally religious country, fewer than one in three Americans—including many liberals—currently believe that the Democratic Party is friendly toward religion (more than half believe the Republicans are). And the percentage of self-described Democrats who say they have "no religion" has more than quadrupled since the early 1970s. The practical impact of these trends is nicely described by Stephen Carter in his book *The Dissent of the Governed.* He describes two black evangelical women who changed their affiliation from liberal political groups to conservative Christian organizations, explaining that "they preferred a place that honored their faith and disdained their politics over a place that honored their politics and disdained their faith." It would be a safe bet that these two religious, civically active women were also highly charitable.[22]

Some liberals are aware that the American left's hostility to organized religion presents a major political problem. Yet most attempts to address this problem seem purely cynical. Take, for example, a seminar at the University of California at Berkeley in the summer of 2005 for liberal politicians and activists. It was titled, "I Don't Believe in God, but I Know America Needs a Spiritual Left." Pretending to value religion—or treating it with this sort of instrumentalism—is an insult to people of faith. It will neither win votes nor stop the attrition of religious liberals to the political right, where they can find an authentic spiritual home. In a fundamentally religious, charitable country, a continued liberal slide into secularism and away from charity is not only bad for America but self-destructive for the Democrats.[23]

If liberals persist in their faith in government and antipathy to religion, the Democrats will become not only the party of secularism but also the party of uncharity. In the absence of change, fewer liberal voters will be moved by appeals to give to others, and it will be increasingly acceptable to express blatantly anticharity viewpoints in liberal circles. We could probably expect increasing attacks from the political left on private foundations, on favorable tax treatment for charitable gifts, and on private nonprofits (especially faith-based organizations) providing aid to the needy, education to children, and other services.

I don't think the liberal charity deficit is inevitable. Certain liberal populations (for example, religious liberals) are still exceptionally charitable. This emphasizes the point that there is no inherent schism between liberal social values and personal charitable giving. And this makes sense, of course: Support for gay marriage, opposition to American military policy, and most other liberal beliefs (besides forced income redistribution to achieve greater income equality) have no logical connection whatsoever to whether one gives and volunteers for good causes, or gives up his seat on the bus, or gives back extra change to a cashier. What I am calling for, then, is not a wholesale rejection of core progressive values—liberals should still be liberals—but rather a selective rejection of the forces that weaken personal generosity. I am asking liberals to stand up for charity.

—

What is so special about America? Is there an essential, uniquely "American" character trait? One prominent historian claims that this characteristic is mass consumerism, which defines the American landscape (and also lies behind international hostility toward the United States). Another author calls the United States "a Promised Land of profit, glory and unfettered growth."[24]

These characterizations may be accurate, but neither one captures our most salient trait. The truly extraordinary thing about the United States is not how much we produce (there are lots of rich, productive countries), nor how much we consume (every country would consume as we do—if only they could). Rather, it is how much we give. America is a land of *charity*.

Mostly a land of charity, that is. From the outside, average American giving levels are unparalleled. However, as we now know, there is a bright cultural line inside our nation. On one side are the majority of citizens who are charitable in all sorts of formal and informal ways—so charitable that they make America exceptional by international standards. On the other side of the line, however, is a sizeable minority who are conspicuously uncharitable. We have identified the reasons these two groups are so different, and they are controversial reasons: One group is religious, the other secular; one supports government income redistribution, the other does not; one works, the other accepts income from the government; one has strong, intact families, the other does not.

If charity were just another virtue—like good manners—this book would be little more than a bit of "culture wars" entertainment, and I wouldn't have written it. But charity is no ordinary virtue: It is critical for the provision of services all across the American economy, from religion to poverty relief to environmental protection. But even beyond what charity supports, it is an essential ingredient in our prosperity, health, happiness, and freedom. Charitable America improves life for all of us. Selfish America makes us all worse off.

So it is in all of our interest—conservative and liberal, religious and secular—to protect the great tradition of giving we have, and to expand the ranks of givers. There should not be "two Americas" when it comes to charity. Our challenge is to make this story untrue.

Appendix

THE DATA ON CHARITY
AND SELFISHNESS

This book—or any book that seeks to reach conclusions about the world on the basis of statistics—is as useful and accurate only as the data and statistical analysis on which the conclusions are based. There is a huge amount of data and analysis lurking behind the preceding chapters, the details on which I did not dwell in the main discussion. Some of the discussion (particularly on statistical modeling procedures) is in the endnotes. But most details I have skipped for the sake of brevity and readability, and on the excellent advice of my editor and others. However, rather than ask all readers to take my analyses on faith, this appendix discusses the ten datasets I used most intensively in this project. I introduce each dataset in turn, describe how I used it, and present some of the most salient results that appear in the text.

This appendix is far from exhaustive, not only in the data I describe but also with respect to the statistics and procedures I summarize. To describe every data source and explain every statistical test that went into the analysis in this book would make for an appendix nearly as long as the book itself. Instead, I have selected here the data summaries and statistical tests that are particularly important for building the book's arguments.

Most of the data I used came from surveys conducted of individuals over the past decade. These surveys usually entailed asking someone (in person, on the phone, or through the mail) something like, "Did you give money to any charities or causes last year?" These surveys provide a marvelous resource for understanding charitable behavior because they generally look at large numbers of individuals (instead of aggregating across groups of people) and get the information straight from respondents. This is especially important in understanding charitable behavior, for three reasons. First, this is the only way to get at the nonmoney giving (volunteering, giving informally to family and friends, etc.) that characterizes so much of American charity, information that is lost when we look only at government-collected statistics on official money charity. Second, we can match up giving decisions with people's personal characteristics: their political views, religious beliefs, attitudes about the government, family circumstances, and demographics. Third, surveys of individuals are less likely than "official" (usually government) data to leave out key populations. For example, if we relied exclusively on data on charitable donations from the Internal Revenue Service, we would know only about the gifts people report to benefit from tax deductions. This would effectively cut off the bottom of the income distribution, an unwise move if we really seek to understand charity in America.

Survey data are, therefore, a blessing for researchers like me—especially when they are collected by highly reliable, professional sources (as all the data used in this book are). But these data still are not perfect. Four problems beset survey-based data analysis. The first problem is that the way questions are asked sometimes biases the way people answer the questions, which in turn leads to a systematic over- or underestimate of the phenomenon at hand. For example, imagine I asked you about your charitable giving in the following two ways:

1. "Do you agree that the government has a basic responsibility to take care of people who can't take care of themselves?"
2. "What do you think about federal spending on welfare? Are we spending too little, just right, or too much?"

These questions get at a similar principle—government money to aid citizens in financial need—but do so in very different ways. The first talks about the need, the second about the money. And so we would expect to find (and do find, when questions are asked in these ways) that people are far more likely to agree with the first question, and to say "too much" to the second.

The second problem with survey data is that a lot of people either refuse to answer certain questions or answer "don't know." If certain people tend to answer this way, or tend to give this instead of answers they don't care to give, the data may not reflect reality. I have found in the past that survey data on charity can suffer from this sort of problem. Specifically, nonresponses to giving questions tend to vary systematically in some surveys by respondents' incomes, education levels, race, and age.[1]

The third problem we often face is that a survey might not really represent a population. For example, a survey about religious beliefs conducted in rural Alabama would not reflect beliefs across the United States as a whole. Many surveys are unrepresentative in less obvious ways than this, though. For charitable giving, we would be worried about a survey of giving behavior conducted a few weeks after a major humanitarian disaster, such as September 11, 2001, the 2004 tsunami, or hurricane Katrina in 2005, because at these times people tend to give far more than usual.

Finally, whenever a survey asks people about their "virtue," we have to worry about the veracity of responses. It may be hard for people to admit that they don't give and volunteer, and some may elect to say they give when they do not.

Researchers meet these threats, as I do here, primarily with the force of replication. It is unwise to rely on a single dataset to answer all one's questions. Indeed, it is not especially wise to use a single dataset to answer even one question because of the problems I have just discussed. The data gathering for this book involved assembling so many large databases for this reason—in which different surveyors at different times asked different populations similar questions (but in different ways). Although individual surveys and populations might produce inaccuracies and biases, a large body of evidence on a topic is more trustworthy. I am confident in the findings in this book because so many data sources brought me to the same conclusions.

When dealing with relationships between charity and other forces, a problem that often arises is one of controlling for alternative explanations. In chapter 1, I found that political conservatives give more to charity than political liberals. It is tempting to conclude that political orientation is responsible for differences in charitable giving, but that would be mostly incorrect. The true explanation is that there are forces that affect political views and the tendency to give, and these forces are the real explanation for the politics-charity relationship observed in the data.

Statisticians have developed a set of techniques to get to the truth of these kinds of relationships, and these techniques are called *regression analyses*. Readers will note that, when I find a relationship between two variables, say between religious participation and giving, I usually go an extra step and isolate this relationship by holding all other factors constant. Regression analysis allows me to do this, giving the true association between charity and religion. The technical details of the specific regression analyses I use in this book are contained in the end notes. However, I will also provide the details on a few key regressions in this appendix.

Even beyond the association between two variables, we sometimes need accurate information about *causation*. In chapter 7, for example, I presented abundant evidence that charitable behavior was associated with economic prosperity, but many questions arose about which variable caused the other—did economic growth stimulate private giving, giving lead to growth, both, or neither? Statistical techniques exist to help resolve issues of causation. The techniques I use for economic prosperity and giving are detailed in this appendix, as well as in the notes to chapter 7.

The Panel Study of Income Dynamics

A valuable data resource for understanding patterns in both giving and receiving charity is the Population Panel of Income Dynamics (PSID), a national panel survey that has been conducted almost annually since 1968. In 2001 and 2003, the Center on Philanthropy at Indiana University sponsored a module of questions on charitable behavior. The survey asked more than 7,000 families different combinations of questions on a broad range of issues, including inquiries about the receipt of unearned income (such as welfare support and gifts from private charities) and the disbursement of gifts. It asked detailed questions about charitable donations of time and money. The PSID is particularly geared toward understanding issues such as poverty and welfare reform. As such, it contains a disproportionate number of low-income respondents, making it especially appropriate for understanding the ways that different types of income affect giving and volunteering by the poor (the subject of chapter 4).

In chapter 1, the calculations on how much Americans volunteer came from the 2003 PSID.

In chapter 4, giving information about welfare recipients, working poor families, and families not on welfare came from the 2003 PSID.

TABLE 1   American Charitable Volunteering, 2003

	Average Volunteering per Household (Hours per Year)	Percentage of All Hours Volunteered
All charities and causes	45.8	100.0
Religious organizations	17.9	39.0
Youth organizations	13.4	29.3
Senior citizens' organizations	2.4	5.1
Health organizations	2.1	4.7
Organizations to help the poor	3.2	6.9
Political organizations or advocacy	1.6	3.4
Other organizations	5.3	11.6

NOTE: N=7,669. SOURCE: PSID.

TABLE 2   Charity from Poor Welfare and Working Poor Families, 2003

	Average Amount Donated	Percent Giving	Average Hours Volunteered	Percent Volunteering
Welfare families[a]	$145	19	42	12
Working poor families[b]	$519	42	47	21

NOTE: N=1,075. SOURCE: PSID.
[a] Welfare families are defined as families receiving welfare support in the bottom income quintile among families in the 2003 PSID with a positive amount of income.
[b] Working poor families are defined as families in the bottom income quintile among families in the 2003 PSID with a positive amount of income.

TABLE 3   Giving from All Families Receiving Welfare Support, Versus Families Not Receiving Any Welfare, 2003

Type of Giving	Percentage of Families Not Receiving Welfare That Give	Percentage of Families Receiving Welfare That Give
Religious organizations	30	15
Combination organizations (United Ways, etc.)	12	4
Organizations to help the poor	18	6
Health organizations	10	4
Education organizations	7	3
Youth organizations	6	2
Arts and culture organizations	4	2
Community development organizations	3	2
Environmental organizations	3	1
International organizations	2	1

NOTE: N=7,644. SOURCE: PSID.

TABLE 4   Giving Money, Volunteering, and Welfare Support in 2001 and 2003

	Family Received Welfare Support in 2001	Family Did Not Receive Welfare Support in 2001
Family received welfare support in 2003	Percentage giving money: 20 Percentage volunteering: 9	Percentage giving money: 27 Percentage volunteering: 15
Family did not receive welfare support in 2003	Percentage giving money: 29 Percentage volunteering: 16	Percentage giving money: 64 Percentage volunteering: 23

NOTE: N=7,420. SOURCE: PSID.

Chapter 4 compares the probabilities of giving money and volunteering for families that were on welfare in 2001 and 2003, those that were not, as well as families that went on or off welfare in that period. These data matched families in the 2001 and 2003 PSID samples.

The Social Capital Community Benchmark Survey

A major and important data source for charitable and civic activity is the Social Capital Community Benchmark Survey (SCCBS). The SCCBS was undertaken from July 2000 to February 2001 by researchers at various American universities in collaboration with the Roper Center for Public Opinion Research and the

Saguaro Seminar at Harvard University's Kennedy School of Government. The intent of the survey was to expose various hypotheses about civil society and charitable behavior to empirical scrutiny. The SCCBS contained three types of questions. First, attitudes of individuals about their communities were probed. Second, respondents were asked about their "civic behavior," including their participation in voluntary community activities—including, specifically, whether they gave and volunteered for religious and nonreligious charities, and if so, how much. Finally, the survey collected a full battery of sociodemographic measures for each respondent. The data consist of nearly 30,000 observations drawn from forty-one communities across twenty-nine states, as well as a nationwide sample.

I use the SCCBS data most intensively in chapter 2, which looks at the relationship between giving and religious participation.

In chapter 2, I use the SCCBS data to estimate the isolated effects of religious participation and other variables on giving decisions. Note that the religion variables are large and highly significant. Also note the politics variables: In the binary model, liberals and conservatives are not distinguishable (t-statistic of the test that they are equivalent: 1.26); in the continuous model, conservatives are slightly (but distinguishably) more generous than liberals (t-statistic: 4.23).

TABLE 5 Giving and Volunteering Among Religious People and Secularists, 2000

	People Who Attend Their House of Worship Nearly Every Week or More Often	People Who Attend a House of Worship Less Than a Few Times per Year, or Have No Religion
Percentage giving money to charity each year	91	66
Percentage volunteering each year	67	44
Value of annual charitable gifts	$2,210	$642
Number of occasions volunteered	12	5.8
Percentage giving money to secular charities each year	71	61
Percentage volunteering for secular causes each year	60	39
Value of annual charitable gifts to secular charities	$532	$467

NOTE: N=29,233. SOURCE: SCCBS.

TABLE 6   Variables That Individually Affect the Probability of Giving and Size of Gifts to Charity, 2000

Variable	Dependent Variable: Respondent Gives at Least Once per Year Probit Coefficient (Standard Error) [Marginal Value]	Dependent Variable: Value of Respondent's Annual Gifts Tobit Coefficient (Standard Error) [Marginal Value]
Constant	-0.493* (0.066) [-0.099]	-2,506.22*(87.371) [-1,832.121]
Religious	0.384* (0.03) [0.077]	1,130.4*(30.267) [826.355]
Secular	-0.656* (0.025) [-0.132]	-761.311* (32.777) [-556.542]
Male	-0.053 (0.022) [-0.011]	192.621* (26.2) [140.812]
Married	0.103* (0.024) [0.021]	168.617* (29.148) [123.264]
Family size	0.0018 (0.0076) [0.0004]	21.6851 (9.5235) [15.8525]
Age	0.0074* (0.0007) [0.0015]	15.8724* (0.8943) [11.6032]
Family income ($1,000s)	0.0108* (0.0005) [0.0022]	26.3097* (0.5147) [19.2332]
High school graduate[a]	0.447* (0.038) [0.09]	554.594* (57.721) [405.425]
College graduate[a]	0.788* (0.047) [0.159]	991.475* (63.769) [724.799]
Attended graduate school[a]	0.929* (0.055) [0.187]	1,313.74*(67.682) [960.386]
White[b]	0.285* (0.03) [0.057]	442.544* (39.269) [323.514]
Black[b]	0.14* (0.039) [0.028]	513.696* (50.917) [375.528]
Politically conservative[c]	0.024 (0.027) [0.005]	271.631* (31.287) [198.57]
Politically liberal[c]	0.059 (0.028) [0.012]	127.606* (34.064) [93.284]

NOTE: N=23,029. SOURCE: SCCBS.
Significance: * Coefficient is significant at the 0.01 level or higher.
[a] Reference group: No high school diploma.
[b] Reference group: Nonblack minority.
[c] Reference group: Politically centrist.

TABLE 7   Giving and Volunteering Among Religious, Secular, Conservative, and Liberal Populations, 2000

	Religious Conservatives	Secular Liberals	Religious Liberals	Secular Conservatives
Population percentage	19.1	10.5	6.4	7.3
Percentage giving money to charity each year	91	72	91	63
Average value of annual charitable gifts	$2,367	$741	$2,123	$661
Percentage giving money to religious causes each year	88	22	86	34
Percentage giving money to nonreligious causes each year	71	69	72	55
Percentage volunteering each year	67	52	67	37
Average number of occasions volunteered	11.9	7.2	12.6	4.7
Percentage volunteering for religious causes each year	62	51	60	35
Percentage volunteering for nonreligious causes each year	60	47	63	31

NOTE: N=29,233. SOURCE: SCCBS.

Chapter 2 also looks at the intersection of religion and politics.

TABLE 8   Measures of Charitable Giving, by Income Class, 2000

Annual Household Income	Average Value of Annual Charitable Gifts	Percentage Giving Money to Charity Each Year	Percentage Giving Money to Religious Causes Each Year	Percentage Giving Money to Nonreligious Causes Each Year	Average Annual Gifts as a Percentage of Income
0–$20,000	$458	64	52	44	4.58
$20,001–$30,000	$710	75	60	56	2.84
$30,001–$50,000	$1,093	84	67	69	2.73
$50,001–$75,000	$1,530	89	72	78	2.45
$75,001–$100,000	$2,059	92	73	83	2.35
$100,001 and above	$3,089	94	74	89	3.09

NOTE: N=26,062. SOURCE: SCCBS.

TABLE 9   Two-Stage Least Squares Estimates of Private Charity Effect on Income

Independent Variable	Instrumental Variables Regression Dependent Variable: Income Coefficient (Standard Error)	Instrumental Regression (OLS) Dependent Variable: Money Gifts Coefficient (Standard Error)
Intercept	-640 (1,631)	-1,622* (102)
Money gifts per year	3.70* (0.487)	–
Volunteer times per year	–	21.61* (0.758)
Religious	-5,206* (609)	886* (27)
Secular	507 (448)	-414* (28)
Male	4,306* (351)	363* (23)
Married	11,031* (403)	391* (25)
Household size	1,629* (118)	56.4* (8.1)
Age	786* (55)	33.79* (3.76)
Age squared	-9.7* (0.5)	-0.259* (0.038)
High school graduate	15,436* (714)	512* (46)
College graduate	27,640* (940)	1,118* (51)
Graduate school	32,728* (1,137)	1,569* (54)
White	4,760* (520)	401* (33)
Black	-718 (648)	435* (44)
Politically conservative	-2,061* (395)	224* (27)
Politically liberal	248 (414)	80* (30)
R^2	0.35	0.24
N	22,925	24,265

* Coefficient is significant at the 0.05 level or above. SOURCE: SCCBS.

Chapter 4 uses the SCCBS to look at the relationship between charitable giving and income.

The SCCBS is the basis for some of the statistics in chapter 7 about the connections between prosperity and charitable behavior. For example, the effect of money giving on household income

TABLE 10   Charity and Self-Judged Happiness and Health, 2000

	Volunteers (%)	Nonvolunteers (%)	Givers (%)	Nongivers (%)
I am:				
Not happy at all	0.4	1.5	0.6	2.1
Not very happy	3	6	4	8
Happy	53	61	55	62
Very happy	44	31	40	28
My health is:				
Poor	2	5	3	6
Fair	7	13	8	13
Good	23	30	25	30
Very Good	40	33	39	30
Excellent	28	20	25	21

NOTE: N=28,834. SOURCE: SCCBS.

comes from a two-stage least squares regression in which volunteering (which only affects income via its relationship to money donations) is used as an instrument for money gifts.

The General Social Survey

The General Social Survey (GSS) is a nationwide survey that has been administered through the National Opinion Research Center (NORC) most years since 1972. It asks a sample of about 2,000 respondents different subsets of about 4,000 questions on a wide variety of topics. Like the PSID and SCCBS, the GSS collects a large amount of sociodemographic information on each respondent. Each year, it features batteries of questions on special topics; these have occasionally included giving and volunteering, most notably in 1996 and 2002. In 1996, respondents were asked how much money they donated to charities of many different types. In 2002, the survey probed formal and informal giving.

Chapter 1 uses the 2002 GSS to establish a link between formal charitable giving and informal charitability.

TABLE 11   Formal and Informal Giving, 2002

Percentage of People Who at Least Once per Year	People Who Donate Money to Charity Each Year	People Who Do Not Donate Money to Charity Each Year
Give blood	18	8
Help a homeless person with money or food	67	48
Let someone cut ahead in line	89	76
Give up seat to another person	43	36
Give directions to stranger	90	78
Express concern for the less fortunate	73	66
Return mistaken change to a cashier	51	33

NOTE: N=1,336. SOURCE: GSS.

TABLE 12   Religious Participation and Informal Giving, 2002

Percentage of People Who at Least Once per Year	People Who Attend Religious Services Almost Every Week or More	People Who Attend Services Less than Once per Year, or Have No Religion
Give blood	18	11
Help a homeless person with money or food	67	57
Let someone cut ahead in line	86	81
Express concern for the less fortunate	79	64
Return mistaken change to a cashier	52	39

NOTE: N=1,333. SOURCE: GSS.

TABLE 13   Average Annual Giving Levels and Opinions About Government Income Redistribution, 1996

	"The Government Has a Responsibility to Reduce Income Inequality"				
	Agree Strongly	Agree	Neither	Disagree	Disagree Strongly
All gifts	$140	$320	$398	$978	$1,637
Secular gifts only	$66	$139	$132	$389	$591
Religious giving	$113	$229	$317	$598	$903
Health	$11	$18	$21	$32	$96
Education	$8	$21	$32	$61	$140
Social welfare	$12	$45	$21	$76	$54
Environment	$5	$7	$5	$23	$19
Arts	$6	$20	$3	$19	$27
International aid	$2	$2	$1	$3	$20

NOTE: N=1,109. SOURCE: GSS.

Chapter 2 links religious participation to informal charity using the 2002 GSS.

Chapter 3 uses the 1996 GSS to compare the giving of people with different attitudes about government income redistribution.

TABLE 14 Variables That Individually Affect the Probability of Giving and Size of Gifts to Charity, 1996

Independent Variable	Dependent Variable: Respondent Gives at Least Once per Year	Dependent Variable: Value of Respondent's Annual Gifts	Dependent Variable: Value of Respondent's Annual Nonreligious Gifts
Constant	Probit Coefficient (Standard Error) [Marginal Value]	Tobit Coefficient (Standard Error) [Marginal Value]	Tobit Coefficient (Standard Error) [Marginal Value]
Constant	-1.399** (0.477) [-0.515]	-4,121.7*** (1,097.6) [-1,807.3]	-2,458.4*** (513.5) [-850.5]
Disagrees with redistribution	0.277** (0.118) [0.102]	599.4** (274.1) [262.8]	280.2** (122.5) [96.9]
Secular[b]	-0.335** (0.133) [-0.124]	-593.9* (337.5) [-260.4]	23.3 (146.5) [8.1]
Religious[b]	0.493*** (0.149) [0.182]	1,453.9*** (315.9) [637.5]	75.8 (145.6) [26.2]
Age	0.02*** (0.005) [0.007]	23.8** (11.4) [10.5]	10.3** (5.2) [3.6]
Income ($1,000s)	0.008** (0.003) [0.003]	39.6*** (7) [17.4]	18.4*** (3.1) [6.4]
Education (years)	0.0777** (0.0243) [0.0286]	110.87* (56.8) [48.62]	54.74** (25.22) [18.94]
Male	0.011 (0.115) [0.004]	-141.4 (271.4) [-62]	-60.6 (121.4) [-21]
Married	0.077 (0.115) [0.028]	353.2 (268.6) [154.9]	75.3 (120.3) [26]
White[c]	-0.439 (0.317) [-0.162]	-340.4 (683.9) [-149.3]	168 (321.1) [58.1]
Black[c]	-0.421 (0.361) [-0.155]	-404.7 (792.3) [-177.4]	365.8 (366.7) [126.5]
Liberal[d]	-0.15 (0.161) [-0.055]	-367 (386.7) [-160.9]	-214.9 (176.5) [-74.3]
Conservative[d]	-0.047 (0.152) [-0.017]	-364.4 (358.7) [-159.8]	67.1 (156.7) [23.2]

NOTE: N=590. SOURCE: GSS.
Significance: *** Coefficient is significant at the 0.01 level or higher.
** Coefficient is significant at the 0.05 level or higher.
* Coefficient is significant at the 0.10 level or higher.
[a] Disagrees or disagrees strongly that "the government has a responsibility to reduce income inequality."
[b] Reference group: Attends religious services less than every week but more than once per year.
[c] Reference group: Nonblack minority.
[d] Reference group: Politically centrist.

In chapter 3, I use the 1996 GSS data to estimate the isolated effects of opinions about income distribution and other variables on giving decisions. Note that the income redistribution variable is significant, and that the variables for political ideology are not.

Chapter 5 uses the 2002 GSS to look at self-reported happiness among people of different political views and marital statuses.

TABLE 15   Self-Reported Happiness, Political Views, and Marital Status

	Percentage Saying They Are Very Happy in Life
Conservatives	36
Liberals	28
Married	41
Widowed	22
Divorced	16
Separated	17
Never married	26

NOTE: N=1,329. SOURCE: GSS.

The International Social Survey Program

The International Social Survey Program (ISSP) is a program of international survey research collaboration that began in 1983. The ISSP group develops modules dealing with specific topics and adds them to the regular national surveys of some thirty countries worldwide (including the GSS in the United States); although the countries change somewhat from year to year, they always emphasize Europe and North America. The topics in 1996, 1998, and 2002 lent themselves to the research in this book: In 1996, the ISSP focused on the role of government in society; in 1998, it looked at religious participation and also asked respondents about their volunteering; and in 2002, it probed attitudes about family and gender roles. In addition to the topical modules, the ISSP collects full data on the sociodemographic characteristics of respondents.

Chapter 6 uses the 1998 ISSP to describe basic country differences in volunteering.

Chapter 6 compares the United States and Western Europe for religious participation and attitudes on family, using the 2002 ISSP.

Chapter 6 uses the 1996 ISSP to compare attitudes on government income redistribution.

TABLE 16 International Volunteering Comparisons, 1998

Country	Population Percentage Volunteering Annually for All Types of Causes	Population Percentage Volunteering Annually for Nonreligious Causes
United States	51	41
Latvia	39	36
Slovak Republic	38	32
France	37	34
Poland	36	32
Netherlands	36	32
Norway	36	33
Slovenia	34	30
Sweden	32	29
Czech Republic	31	28
Switzerland	30	24
Great Britain	28	24
Ireland	27	24
Portugal	24	17
Bulgaria	23	21
Russia	20	19
Italy	20	14
Hungary	20	16
Western Germany	19	12
Spain	18	15
Denmark	18	14
Austria	18	13
Eastern Germany	13	10

NOTE: N=27,742. SOURCE: ISSP.

TABLE 17 International Comparisons of Religious Behavior and Attitudes on Family, 1998

Country	Population Percentage That Never Practices a Religion	Population Percentage That Attends Worship Services Every Week	Population Percentage That Disagrees It Is Best to Marry If One Wants Kids	Population Percentage That Believes Divorce Is Best Solution to Marriage Problems
Great Britain	63	13	30	62
Netherlands	56	9	57	74
Eastern Germany	53	4	39	81
France	51	7	45	60
Sweden	31	3	42	55
Norway	31	4	38	56
Switzerland	29	9	40	68
Spain	26	19	55	81
Western Germany	24	11	34	74
Denmark	21	2	39	69
Austria	20	22	38	83
United States	19	31	19	43
Ireland	4	62	34	61

NOTE: N=18,484. SOURCE: ISSP.

TABLE 18 International Comparisons of Attitudes
on Government Income Redistribution, 1996

Country	Population Percentage That Believes the Government Has a Responsibility to Reduce Income Differences
Slovenia	80
Poland	78
Spain	77
Eastern Germany	76
Russia	74
France	68
Hungary	67
Ireland	66
Italy	65
Czech Republic	60
Sweden	60
Norway	57
Cyprus	55
United Kingdom	54
Latvia	51
Western Germany	49
United States	33

NOTE: N=23,260. SOURCE: ISSP.

In chapter 6, I use the 1998 ISSP data to estimate the effects of religious participation and other variables on the decision to volunteer for nonreligious charities. Note that the difference between a religious person and a secularist, controlling for other demographics and country of residence, is about $8 - (-9) = 17$ percentage points. Note also that the country fixed effects—which measure the amount that citizens from these countries tend to differ from America in the propensity to volunteer—are significant for most countries and negative in all significant cases. (See Table 19.)

Arts and Religion Survey

The Arts and Religion Survey (ARS) was conducted in 1999 by Princeton Professor Robert Wuthnow and the Gallup Organization. This national, random survey interviewed 1,530 Americans in their homes about their creative and arts-related activities; their

TABLE 19   Variables That Individually Affect the Probability of Giving
and Size of Gifts to Charity, 1996

Dependent Variable: Respondent Volunteers at Least Once per Year for Nonreligious Causes	
Independent Variable	*Probit Coefficient (Standard Error) [Marginal Value]*
Constant	-0.32* (0.05) [-0.09]
Religious[a]	0.28* (0.03) [0.08]
Secular[a]	-0.29* (0.02) [-0.09]
Male	-0.016 (0.02) [-0.005]
Married	0.0212 (0.0204) [0.0062]
Age	0.0016 (0.0006) [0.0005]
Education (years)	0.0002 (0.0004) [0.0001]
Income ($10,000s)	-0.00093 (0.00128) [-0.00027]
Western Germany[b]	-0.9* (0.07) [-0.26]
Eastern Germany[b]	-0.93* (0.11) [-0.27]
Great Britain[b]	-0.32* (0.07) [-0.09]
Austria[b]	-1.15* (0.07) [-0.33]
Hungary[b]	-0.75* (0.07) [-0.22]
Italy[b]	-1* (0.07) [-0.29]
Ireland[b]	-0.7* (0.06) [-0.21]
Netherlands[b]	-0.12 (0.05) [-0.04]
Norway[b]	0.003 (0.055) [0.001]
Sweden[b]	-0.23* (0.06) [-0.07]
Czech Republic[b]	-0.23* (0.06) [-0.07]
Slovenia[b]	-0.23* (0.06) [-0.07]
Poland[b]	-0.35* (0.06) [-0.1]
Russia[b]	-0.52* (0.05) [-0.15]
Spain[b]	-0.93* (0.06) [-0.27]
Latvia[b]	-0.03 (0.06) [-0.01]
Slovak Republic[b]	-0.3* (0.06) [-0.09]
France[b]	-0.09 (0.06) [-0.03]
Cyprus[b]	-0.02 (0.06) [-0.01]
Portugal[b]	-0.87* (0.06) [-0.26]
Denmark[b]	-0.85* (0.07) [-0.25]
Switzerland[b]	-0.71* (0.07) [-0.21]

NOTE: N=22,112. SOURCE: ISSP.

Significance: * Coefficient is significant at the 0.01 level or higher.

[a] Reference group: Attends worship services at least once per year but less than weekly.

[b] Reference group: United States.

attitudes toward the arts; their religious activities, behavior, beliefs, and affiliations; their attitudes toward religion and spirituality; and their involvement in charitable activities. It also collected
a full set of demographics on respondents. This survey is particularly useful for this book because it asked respondents about religious activities and beliefs far beyond simple church attendance.

TABLE 20   Religious Behaviors and Charitable Giving, 1999

	Percentage Giving Money to All Charities	Percentage Giving Money to Religious Causes	Percentage Giving Money to Nonreligious Causes
All people	75	64	50
People who pray every day	83	79	51
People who never pray	53	23	44
People who devote "a great deal of effort" to their spiritual lives	88	84	52
People who devote "no effort" to their spiritual lives	46	20	41
People who belong to a house of worship	88	86	53
People who do not belong to a house of worship	56	32	45
People who attend their house of worship every week	92	92	51
People who never attend a house of worship	42	13	37

NOTE: N=1,252. SOURCE: ARS.

Chapter 2 uses the Arts and Religion Survey to study the association between giving and various religious activities.

Chapter 5 uses the data to see how religious behavior as a child is correlated with adult charity.

TABLE 21   Childhood Church Attendance and Adult Charity

	All People		People Who Never Attend a House of Worship	
Frequency of Attendance at House of Worship As a Child	Percentage Giving Money to All Charities as Adults	Percentage Giving Money to Nonreligious Causes as Adults	Percentage Giving Money to All Charities as Adults	Percentage Giving Money to Nonreligious Causes as Adults
Every week	78	51	47	40
Almost every week	76	48	41	37
Once or twice a month	74	45	48	41
A few times a year	62	51	35	32
Never	56	53	26	29

NOTE: N=1,252. SOURCE: ARS.

Giving USA

Each year, the Giving USA Foundation in Illinois conducts a survey of charitable giving in America in collaboration with the Indiana Center on Philanthropy. The results from the survey form the basis for estimating the aggregate levels of formal charitable giving in America. These data are considered to be the most accurate and authoritative source for American charitable giving statistics—far more accurate than the estimates produced by the U.S. Internal Revenue Service (which counts only contributions to charities that are deducted from income taxes). The Giving USA data allow us to look at how American giving has increased since the mid-1950s, when the data were first collected.

In chapters 1 and 7, changes in real charitable giving and American GDP are compared over time. Table 22 gives the data that form the basis for this comparison.

Chapter 7 establishes a causal relationship between individual giving and GDP per capita by performing Granger tests on the data in Table 22. These tests look at the extent to which prior years' values of one variable predict future values of another variable. We are interested in whether current and three prior years' values of giving predict current GDP, and vice versa. The tests also correct for cumulative effects of variables on themselves by including lagged values of the dependent variables in the models. Restricted F-tests make it possible to reject the hypothesis that the current and lagged values of each variable (together) do not predict the current values of the other variable, in which case we would say that each variable "Granger causes" the other. This is not the same thing as "proving" true mutual causality between variables, but provides a very believable case that causality does exist.[2]

TABLE 22   Inflation-Adjusted Charitable Giving and U.S. GDP, 1954–2004

Year	Real Charitable Giving*	Charitable Giving per Capita	Real GDP*	GDP per Capita
1954	$43.37	$222.14	$2,624	$16,094
1955	$49.53	$247.89	$2,880	$17,356
1956	$55.01	$269.62	$3,027	$17,920
1957	$57.10	$278.57	$3,097	$18,006
1958	$58.80	$284.75	$3,030	$17,325
1959	$66.42	$311.71	$3,240	$18,222
1960	$69.85	$320.46	$3,334	$18,451
1961	$72.65	$321.41	$3,391	$18,463
1962	$73.03	$327.30	$3,621	$19,410
1963	$80.05	$349.61	$3,769	$19,917
1964	$81.51	$349.51	$3,982	$20,752
1965	$87.32	$361.10	$4,274	$21,999
1966	$91.96	$368.59	$4,597	$23,386
1967	$95.86	$379.88	$4,695	$23,629
1968	$102.38	$399.13	$4,950	$24,665
1969	$107.48	$408.89	$5,126	$25,290
1970	$103.08	$386.84	$5,094	$24,842
1971	$109.07	$395.28	$5,252	$25,290
1972	$110.13	$415.84	$5,589	$26,629
1973	$111.25	$421.18	$6,023	$28,424
1974	$106.83	$401.41	$5,965	$27,894
1975	$101.52	$387.28	$5,813	$26,914
1976	$106.09	$402.09	$6,075	$27,864
1977	$111.47	$424.76	$6,431	$29,200
1978	$114.29	$427.34	$6,803	$30,565
1979	$116.90	$440.85	$6,959	$30,921
1980	$115.76	$425.55	$6,655	$29,223
1981	$117.68	$425.72	$6,666	$28,986
1982	$116.09	$402.87	$6,401	$27,568
1983	$119.70	$420.75	$6,694	$28,569
1984	$124.64	$434.17	$7,148	$30,242
1985	$125.85	$422.47	$7,396	$31,014
1986	$140.67	$471.09	$7,524	$31,267
1987	$136.90	$442.63	$7,898	$32,530
1988	$140.92	$457.17	$8,177	$33,372
1989	$150.33	$491.24	$8,395	$33,939
1990	$146.12	$470.98	$8,436	$33,726
1991	$144.36	$457.41	$8,237	$32,492
1992	$149.92	$457.82	$8,474	$32,986
1993	$151.77	$459.10	$8,627	$33,147
1994	$152.38	$444.89	$8,936	$33,921
1995	$152.40	$440.82	$9,119	$34,210
1996	$166.85	$478.43	$9,372	$34,753
1997	$189.73	$529.75	$9,683	$35,480
1998	$202.62	$574.23	$10,064	$36,448
1999	$228.53	$624.07	$10,454	$37,430
2000	$252.03	$677.91	$10,779	$38,165
2001	$244.41	$638.58	$10,664	$37,345
2002	$244.40	$634.25	$10,924	$37,852
2003	$241.29	$630.28	$11,216	$38,407
2004	$248.52	$636.53	$11,728	$39,725

NOTE: All figures are inflation adjusted using the Consumer Price Index (CPI), and in 2004 prices
* Billions of dollars. SOURCE: Giving USA.

TABLE 23   Granger Tests of the Hypothesis That Charity Growth
Causes GDP Growth, and Vice Versa

Variable	Dependent Variable: Per Capita Charity, Current Year	Dependent Variable: GDP per Capita, Current Year
	Coefficient (Standard Error)	Coefficient (Standard Error)
Constant	-0.44 (0.36)	0.49* (0.21)
Per capita charity, current year		0.31** (0.08)
Per capita charity, one year ago	0.94** (0.16)	-0.23 (0.12)
Per capita charity, two years ago	0.09 (0.22)	-0.16 (0.13)
Per capita charity, three years ago	-0.2 (0.16)	0.19* (0.09)
GDP per capita, current year	0.86** (0.22)	
GDP per capita, one year ago	-0.9* (0.35)	1.11** (0.15)
GDP per capita, two years ago	0.11 (0.36)	-0.27 (0.21)
GDP per capita, three years ago	0.07 (0.23)	0.05 (0.14)
F-test statistic of the hypothesis that the lagged values of donations are all zero	41.75**	4.00*
F-test statistic of the hypothesis that the lagged values of GDP are all zero	4.92*	127.08**

NOTES: N=48. Regressions are estimated using ordinary least squares. All values are of
per capita giving and GDP are converted to their natural logarithms. SOURCE: Giving USA.
Significance: ** Coefficient is significant at the 0.01 level or higher.
* Coefficient is significant at the 0.05 level or higher.

Table 23 details the regressions behind the Granger tests.
These tests are also detailed in the table.

The Maxwell Poll

In the fall of 2004, the Campbell Public Affairs Institute at Syracuse University's Maxwell School undertook a national poll of
about 600 American adults, randomly selected, on issues of civic
participation. The survey asked respondents approximately eighty
questions about their beliefs concerning the conduct of government, their involvement in governmental affairs, and their membership in voluntary associations, including religious groups, fraternal
and special interest organizations, and those dedicated to charitable
activity. The poll also collected data on respondent demographics.[3]

TABLE 24   Political Beliefs and Views on Income Equality

	Liberals	Conservatives
Percentage who believe that income differences in our society today are too large	76	41
Percentage who believe that we have become a society of haves and have-nots	92	51
Percentage who believe that income inequality in our society is a serious problem	67	25
Percentage who believe that the government should do more to reduce inequality	80	27

NOTE: N=541. SOURCE: Maxwell Poll.

Chapter 3 uses the Maxwell Poll data to measure the difference between political liberals and conservatives in attitudes about income inequality.

American National Election Study

The American National Election Study (ANES) survey is conducted biannually by the Center for Political Studies and the Survey Research Center at the University of Michigan. The surveys ask approximately 1,500 respondents questions about social trust, civic engagement, and political participation. Respondents also provide demographic information. One of the ways the ANES surveys gauge public opinion is through the use of "feeling thermometers," or 0–100 scales in which respondents are asked to give their opinions about other groups in society, where 0 denotes the most negative feelings possible for the group in question, and 100 is the most positive.

Chapter 1 uses the 2002 ANES data to compare feeling thermometers between donors and nondonors. (See Table 25.)

Giving and Volunteering in the United States

The Giving and Volunteering in the United States survey (GVS) is a telephone survey conducted for the Independent Sector in

TABLE 25   Charitable Giving and Feeling Thermometers, 2002

	All	Average Thermometer Reading for People Who Donate Money to Charity	Average Thermometer Reading for People Who Do Not Donate Money to Charity
Supreme Court	64	64	60
Congress	58	58	54
The military	75	76	72
Federal government	60	61	56
Blacks	66	67	62
Whites	68	69	64
Conservatives	58	59	50
Liberals	51	51	52
Labor unions	52	53	50
Big business	48	49	47
Poor people	66	66	64
Welfare recipients	53	54	50
Hispanics	63	64	60
Christian fundamentalists	52	53	47
Elderly people	76	77	72
Environmentalists	63	63	61
Gays and lesbians	48	48	48
Catholics	62	63	57
Jews	63	64	57
Protestants	64	66	56
Feminists	54	54	52
Asian Americans	63	64	59
News media	52	52	53
Catholic Church	52	53	47

NOTES: N=1,018. All differences are statistically significant at the 0.05 level except in the case of attitudes toward gays and lesbians. SOURCE: ANES.

2001 with a random national sample of 4,216 adults of twenty-one years or older. The interviews asked about individual volunteering habits in the twelve months prior to the survey and about household giving during the year 2000. In addition, respondents were asked about their informal giving and volunteering, and why they gave and volunteered (or failed to do so). The survey also collects demographic data on respondents.

Chapter 1 details the relationship between formal and informal money and time gifts.

TABLE 26   The Relationship Between Formal and Informal Giving, 2000

	Percentage of These People That Give Money Annually to Friends, Neighbors, or Strangers	Percentage of These People People That Volunteer Time for Friends, Neighbors, or Strangers
People who formally donate money to charities	53	60
People who do not formally donate money to charities	19	43

NOTE: N=4,132. SOURCE: GVS.

TABLE 27   Gifts to 9-11 Causes by Religious and Secular People, 2001

	Among People Who Attend Their House of Worship Every Week or More Often	Among People Who Never Attend a House of Worship, or Have No Religion At All
Percentage that gave money to a 9-11 cause	67	56
Percentage that gave other items (e.g., blood) to a 9-11 cause	28	24
Percentage that volunteered time for a 9-11 cause	10	8

NOTE: N=1,274. SOURCE: America Gives Survey.

America Gives

The America Gives survey was conducted by the Center on Philanthropy at Indiana University around the time of the terrorist attacks of September 11, 2001. Approximately 1,200 adults across the United States were interviewed about their charitable responses to the tragedies, and data were collected on money giving, volunteering, and other types of gifts (such as blood donations).[4]

Chapter 2 lists September 11 related giving as an example of how religious and secular people differ in their charitable responses to even totally secular causes.

Notes

Introduction

1. Mr. Carter made his remark in a speech at St. Olaf's College, Minnesota, February, 2004. See "Americans Oblivious to Suffering," *WorldNetDaily.com Inc.*, February 23, 2004, http://www.worldnetdaily.com/news/article.asp?ARTICLE_ID=37246 (accessed March 22, 2006).

2. Alexis de Tocqueville, *Democracy in America*, ed. J. P. Maier, trans. George Lawrence (Garden City, N.Y.: Anchor Books, 1969), http://xroads.virginia.edu/~hyper/DETOC/ch2_05.htm (accessed March 6, 2006).

3. Sources: 2000 Social Capital Community Benchmark Survey (SCCBS), *Giving USA 2005*, Roper Center for Public Opinion Research (2000), www.roper.com; *Giving USA 2005*, American Association of Fundraising Council (AAFRC), Giving USA Foundation, Center on Philanthropy at Indiana University, 2005. The range of estimates of charitable giving is fairly wide, with some sources finding giving in as few as 50 percent of households, and others finding it in more than 80 percent. Mark O. Wilhelm, a professor at Indiana University-Purdue University, Indianapolis, has compared many giving surveys, and finds 70 percent to be the most common level.

4. Source: *Giving USA 2005*. In his landmark book *Bowling Alone*, Robert Putnam wrote in 2000 that "after 1960 our generosity has steadily shriveled." Putnam's statement was based on a small decline in giving as a percentage of GDP from about 1960 until 1998, when he conducted his research. However, 1960 was a high-water mark in American giving, and giving increases from

the late 1990s to the present have erased the post–1960 decline. Robert D. Putnam, *Bowling Alone: The Collapse and Revival of American Community* (New York: Simon & Schuster, 2000), 123.

5. Source: 2003 Panel Study of Income Dynamics (PSID), Center on Philanthropy Panel Study (COPPS) (2001); in the Panel Study of Income Dynamics Wave XXXII computer file, Ann Arbor, Mich.: ICPSR (http://simba.isr.umich.edu).

6. Sources: 2003 PSID, 2000 SCCBS.

7. Sources: 2002 General Social Survey (GSS), 2000 Giving and Volunteering Survey (GVS). James Allan Davis, Tom W. Smith, and Peter V. Marsden, *General Social Surveys, 1972–2002: Cumulative CodeBook* (Chicago: National Opinion Research Center, 2002); Independent Sector, *Giving and Volunteering in the United States* (GVS) (Washington, D.C.: Independent Sector, 2002), www.IndependentSector.org. Not surprisingly, the differences are the same for people who volunteer formally versus those who do not. For example, volunteers are also 91 percent more likely to give blood, 50 percent more likely to give up their seat on the bus, and 31 percent more likely to help a homeless person.

8. Like and dislike here is measured with "feeling thermometers," where respondents give particular groups and issues scores (ranging from 0 to 100), in which a high score represents a favorable feeling toward members of a particular group, and a low score means the respondent doesn't care for these people. Source: 2002 American National Election Studies (ANES), Center for Political Studies (producer and distributor), University of Michigan, Ann Arbor, Michigan, 2002. In these data, givers and nongivers were equally sympathetic to homosexuals.

9. Source: 2000 GVS.

10. Ibid; Some of the reasons for not giving transcend national boundaries. For example, a survey of Spaniards in 1992 showed that, among those who did not give anything to charity, a very common response was cynicism about the usefulness of one's gift: More than a third of Spanish nongivers said they didn't give because they did not think it would help solve any problems, or would not reach those in need. This cynicism exists in the United States as well. Arthur C. Brooks, "Charitable Giving to Humanitarian Organizations in Spain," *Hacienda Pública Española/Revista de Economía Pública* 165 (February 2003): 9; One American author has explained his own insufficient charity by saying, "The problem will still be there when I am done

giving. The problem will be there if I do not give. So, what difference would my gift make?" Aaron S. Edlin, "The Choose-Your-Charity Tax: A Way to Incentivize Greater Giving," *Economists' Voice* 2, no. 3 (2005), http://www.bepress.com/ev/vol2/iss3/art3 (accessed March 6, 2006).

11. Source: 2000 GVS. The average income in this calculation is the household median of $45,000.

12. William Branigin, "U.S. Consumer Debt Grows at Alarming Rate," *Washington Post,* January 12, 2004. See also the Motley Fool Credit Center, http://www.fool.com/.

13. Source: 2002 GSS. These conclusions come from the marginal effects produced by a probit estimation of the likelihood of giving at least once in 2002.

14. Source: 2002 GSS.

15. Source: 1996 GSS.

16. Source: 2001 PSID. I estimate the likelihood of giving using a logit model, and simulate giving probabilities with the resulting cumulative distribution function, holding the regressors at their mean values except those I am comparing (welfare receipt, marital status, children in the home, and church affiliation).

Chapter One

1. Thomas Lehrer (1965), "The Folk Song Army." *That Was the Year That,* compact disc, Reprise/Wea, 6179, ASIN B000002K07.

2. Bonnie Azab Powell, "Framing the Issues: UC Berkeley Professor George Lakoff Tells How Conservatives Use Language to Dominate Politics," *UC Berkeley News,* October 27, 2003, http://www.berkeley.edu/news/media/releases/2003/10/27_lakoff.shtml (accessed March 6, 2006).

3. Jack Block and Jeanne H. Block, "Nursery School Personality and Political Orientation Two Decades Later," *Journal of Research in Personality* (forthcoming).

4. Jane Smiley, "The Unteachable Ignorance of the Red States," *Slate,* November 4, 2004, http://www.slate.com/id/2109218/ (accessed March 6, 2006).

5. Derrick Z. Jackson, "At Bob Jones U., a Disturbing Lesson About the Real George W.," *Boston Globe,* February 9, 2000; Greg Palast, "Killer, Coward, Con-Man: Good Riddance, Gipper!" *Baltimore Chronicle,* June 6, 2004.

6. Associated Press, "Kerry Invokes His Faith in Discussing Federal Budget," *Boston.com*, November 5, 2005, http://www.boston.com/news/local/massachusetts/articles/2005/11/05/kerry_invokes_his_faith_in_discussing_federal_budget?mode=PF (accessed March 6, 2006); Jonathan Weisman and Alan Cooperman, "A Religious Protest Largely from the Left," *Washington Post*, December 14, 2005.

7. Stephen Goldsmith, "What Compassionate Conservatism Is—And Is Not," *Hoover Digest* 4 (Fall 2000), http://www.hooverdigest.org/004/goldsmith.html (accessed March 6, 2006).

8. Michelle Cottle, "A Way to Voters' Hearts Is Through Their Stomachs?" *New Republic Online*, December 29, 2003, http://www.tnr.com/primary/index.mhtml?pid=1133 (accessed March 6, 2006); Marc Sandalow, "Evoking Compassionate Conservatism," *San Francisco Chronicle*, May 1, 2002; Dan Quayle is quoted in John Micklethwait and Adrian Woolridge, *The Right Nation: Conservative Power in America* (New York: Penguin Books, 2004), 132.

9. Sources: 2000 SCCBS, 2002 GSS. Many datasets yield nearly identical, statistically insignificant results on this point. Laboratory experiments with human subjects find that conservatives and liberals are similarly disposed to give or not. See Lisa Anderson, Jennifer Mellor, and Jeffrey Milyo, "Do Liberals Play Nice? The Effects of Party and Political Ideology in Public Goods and Trust Games" (working paper 0417, Department of Economics, University of Missouri, 2004).

10. Source: 2000 SCCBS. A conservative family earning $25,000 per year was 6 percent more likely to give charitably than a liberal family having the same income; a conservative family earning $50,000 was 3 percent more likely to give; and one earning $100,000 was 2 percent more likely to give.

11. Source: 2002 ANES.

12. Source: 2002 GSS. Some smaller informal giving differences also exist. Liberals are a bit more likely than conservatives to give money to a homeless person, give up their seats on a bus, and give directions to strangers; conservatives are more likely than liberals to return mistaken change to a cashier and express empathy toward needy persons.

13. Sources: 2004 GSS, 2002 GSS, 2000 SCCBS.

14. The national average giving level of 2.8 percent of household income refers to the median level for households that itemize their charitable deductions. Since taxpayers having the lowest incomes seldom itemize, data are only available on income brackets starting in the middle class. This should

artificially inflate liberal giving (because lower-income religious conservatives—who donate at extremely high rates—are overlooked). The electoral and giving maps here are consistent with the *Generosity Index,* an annual ranking of the American states in income donated, which has found that "red states" have generally given more than the "blue states" every year since the ranking has been calculated. G. Jeffrey MacDonald, "Who Are the Nation's 'Cheapstates'? Try the Blue Ones," *Christian Science Monitor,* December 22, 2004, http://www.csmonitor.com/2004/1222/p15s01-ussc.html (accessed March 6, 2006).

15. Source: 2003 PSID. For states giving Mr. Bush 50–59 percent of the vote, the average charitable giving level was 3.1 percent of household income; for states giving him 40–49 percent, it was 2.5 percent. Bush's highest percentages came from Utah (71 percent), Wyoming (69), Idaho (68), Nebraska (67), and Oklahoma (66). His lowest percentages came from the District of Columbia (9 percent), Massachusetts (37), Vermont (39), Rhode Island (39), New York (40), and Maryland (43).

16. Source: 2003 PSID.

17. Source: 2002 GSS.

18. George Bernard Shaw, "Socialism for Millionaires," in *Essays in Fabian Socialism* (London: Constable & Company Ltd., 1949).

19. David Wagner, *What's Love Got to Do with It? A Critical Look at American Charity* (New York: New Press, 2000), 94.

20. Friedrich Schneider and Werner W. Pommerehne, "Free Riding and Collective Action: An Experiment in Public Microeconomics," *Quarterly Journal of Economics* 96, no. 4 (1981): 689.

21. Stephanie Strom, "What Is Charity?" *New York Times,* November 14, 2005, F1.

22. Arthur C. Brooks, "The Way We Give Now," *Wall Street Journal,* November 21, 2005, A16.

Chapter Two

1. Gerard Manley Hopkins, "To Him Who Ever Thought with Love of Me" (1918), in *Poems of Gerard Manley Hopkins,* ed. Robert Bridges (World eBook Library: Project Gutenberg Consortia Center), http://worldebook library.com/eBooks/WorldeBookLibrary.com/hoppoe.htm (accessed March 6, 2006).

2. Average household giving is $1,279 in San Francisco County, and $1,286 in South Dakota. Source: 2000 SCCBS.

3. Sources: 2003 American Community Survey (ACS), U.S. Census, http://www.census.gov/acs/ (accessed March 15, 2006), and 2000 SCCBS. Average income figures are for 2000.

4. Data source: 2000 SCCBS.

5. Malachi 3:10, Luke 6:38. These verses are from the New International Version of the Bible. Bhagawad Gita 18.06; Dhammapada 224. See also Matthew E. Bunson, *The Wisdom Teachings of the Dalai Lama* (New York: Plume, 1997), 76; also Satguru Sivaya Subramuniyaswami, "Kural 242," in *Weaver's Wisdom: Ancient Precepts for a Perfect Life* (Hawaii: Himalayan Academy Publishing, 1999), 65.

6. Source: 2000 SCCBS.

7. These results rely on the marginal effects from probit and tobit estimations of the likelihood of giving, controlling for secularism, religious attendance, and all the other demographics mentioned.

8. There are no data that help us figure out whether churchgoers are more or less likely than nonchurchgoers to inflate their charitable giving in surveys. On the one hand, they might do so because of the perceived pressure to behave charitably as a person of faith. On the other hand, they might be *less* likely than secularists to distort their giving if they feel answerable to a higher power—who presumably is not fooled by a survey response.

9. Source: Robert Wuthnow, *Arts and Religion Survey 1999* (ARS) (Princeton, N.J.: Gallup Organization). The percentage of people devoting "a great deal of effort to their spiritual lives" includes 15 percent of Catholics, 11 percent of Jews, 59 percent of Mormons, 44 percent of Orthodox Christians, 43 percent of Moslems, 28 percent from other religions, and, paradoxically perhaps, even 6 percent of atheists and agnostics.

10. Source: 2000 SCCBS.

11. The number of houses of worship comes from *Religious Congregations and Membership in the United States 2000,* Association of Statisticians of American Religious Bodies (ASARB). The charity levels come from Internal Revenue Service data from 2001. Source: "How Much Taxpayers of Different Income Levels Wrote Off in Charitable Deductions: A State-by-State Breakdown," *Chronicle of Philanthropy,* August 8, 2002.

12. The expert is George McCully of Boston's *Catalog for Philanthropy,* who compiles the annual *Generosity Index,* a ranking of giving by state. See G.

Jeffrey MacDonald, "Who Are the Nation's 'Cheapstates'? Try the Blue Ones," *Christian Science Monitor,* December 22, 2004, http://www. csmonitor.com/2004/1222/p15s01-ussc.html (accessed March 6, 2006).

13. Source: 2000 SCCBS.

14. These results come from the marginal coefficients from probit and tobit estimations of the likelihood of giving and volunteering, and the value of gifts and hours volunteered, controlling for secularism, religious attendance, and all the other relevant demographics. To be careful about measuring fairly whether someone is "religious," let us also look at different kinds of religious and spiritual behavior. Among the population in 1999, people who prayed every day were 16 percent more likely to give to nonreligious charities than people who never prayed, and church members were 18 percent more likely to give than nonmembers. People who devoted "a great deal of effort" to their spirituality were 28 percent more likely to give to secular charities than people who made "no effort." Furthermore, people who thought "beliefs don't matter as long as you're a good person" were 8 percent more likely to give to explicitly secular charities as well. Source: 1999 ARS.

15. Source: 2000 GVS.

16. Source: 2002 GSS.

17. Ibid.

18. Source: 2001 America Gives Survey, Indiana Center on Philanthropy, Indianapolis, 2002.

19. Sources: 2000 GVS, 2000 SCCBS.

20. Gara LaMarche, "Compassionate Aversionism," *Nation,* April 19, 2001, http://www.thenation.com/doc/20010507/lamarche (accessed March 6, 2006).

21. Here's how one atheist writer makes the case that religious giving is a waste of money: "If Christianity were so spectacularly marked by the urge to give to others without asking anything in return, Christian institutions would have done far more than they have. As it is, almost all religious hospitals, clinics, schools, and colleges charge and collect fees that are the same as, or very little different than, similar nonreligious organizations. . . . A reasonable person would conclude that the religiously affiliated schools and hospitals, far from being praiseworthy examples of altruism, are, in fact, inefficient and wasteful of money and resources." Tim Gorski, "Concerning Christian Charity," *Positive Atheism* 1, no. 7 (1999): 7.

22. Matthew 25:45–46 (King James version).

23. Sources: 1999 ARS, 2002 ANES.

24. See http://www.au.org/site/PageServer?pagename=resources_religious right (accessed September 1, 2005).

25. Louis Bolce and Gerald De Maio, "Our Secularist Democratic Party," *Public Interest,* no. 149 (Fall 2002): 12–13; Geoffrey Layman, *The Great Divide: Religious and Cultural Conflict in American Party Politics* (New York: Columbia University Press, 2001).

26. The Pew Forum on Religion and Public Life, "Religion: A Strength and Weakness for Both Parties," The Pew Research Center for the People and the Press, August 30, 2005, http://people-press.org/reports/pdf/254.pdf (accessed March 6, 2006).

27. Adam Wolfson, "One Nation Under God?" *Commentary* 114, no. 3 (2002): 44–49.

28. See Jim VandeHei, "Future of Orthodox Jewish Vote Has Implications for GOP," *Washington Post*, August 3, 2006, A06.

29. Source: 2004 Maxwell Poll on Civic Engagement and Inequality, Campbell Public Affairs Institute (Syracuse, New York: Maxwell School at Syracuse University), (http://www.maxwell.syr.edu/campbell/Poll/Citizenship Poll.htm).

Chapter Three

1. Laura Goren, "What Nadar Said at the NAACP Convention," *Baltimore Chronicle,* August 30, 2000, http://www.baltimorechronicle.com/media_nader_sep00.html (accessed March 31, 2006).

2. Benjamin Franklin, *The Autobiography* (New York: P. F. Collier & Son, 1909–1914). In Franklin's own words, "This condition carried the bill through; for the members, who had [initially] oppos'd the grant, and now conceiv'd they might have the credit of being charitable without the expence, agreed to its passage; and then, in soliciting subscriptions among the people, we urg'd the conditional promise of the law as an additional motive to give, since every man's donation would be doubled; thus the clause work'd both ways."

3. If the idea that proposed or real taxes are a legitimate substitute for charity seems strange to you, you are not alone. The great American judge Learned Hand made the point in 1934: "Anyone may arrange his affairs so that his taxes shall be as low as possible; he is not bound to choose that pattern which best pays the treasury. There is not even a patriotic duty to increase

one's taxes. Over and over again the Courts have said that there is nothing sinister in so arranging affairs as to keep taxes as low as possible. Everyone does it, rich and poor alike and all do right, for nobody owes any public duty to pay more than the law demands. Taxes are enforced exactions, not voluntary contributions." *Helvering V. Gregory,* 60 F.2d 809 (Second Circuit, 1934).

4. Forty-three percent of respondents "disagreed" or "strongly disagreed" that "the government has a responsibility to reduce income inequality." Together, these are the people I refer to simply as those who disagreed. Thirty-three percent "agreed" or "strongly agreed" with this statement; I refer to these people as those who agreed.

5. Source: 1996 GSS.

6. Ibid.

7. Source: 2000 GVS.

8. Sources: 2004 Maxwell Poll, 1996 GSS. To obtain these results, I regressed the giving decision and the amount of gifts on a vector of demographics, and estimated the marginal effects from probit and tobit models.

9. Source: 2002 GSS.

10. Arthur C. Brooks, "Is There a Dark Side to Government Support for Nonprofits?" *Public Administration Review* 60, no. 3 (2000): 211–218.

11. Jonathan Gruber and Daniel M. Hungerman, "Faith-Based Charity and Crowd-Out During the Great Depression" (working paper no. 1132, National Bureau of Economic Research, 2005), http://www.nber.org/papers/W11332 (accessed March 26, 2006).

12. J. Schiff, "Does Government Spending Crowd Out Charitable Contributions?" *National Tax Journal* 38, no. 4 (1985): 535–546. The original analysis here uses a cross section of data from the U.S. states. I regress the logarithm of donations per capita on the log of the average TANF payment, the log of state government spending per capita, the state and local tax revenues as a percentage of total income, and the log of per capita adjusted gross income. I estimate the model using ordinary least squares, and interpret the coefficients as elasticities. Sources: 2001 IRS data, 2002 data from the National Association of State Budget Officers, and 1997 welfare data from the Urban Institute.

13. Those skeptical of this analysis will note that I have not corrected for every difference between New Hampshire and Tennessee that might affect charity. It would not be possible, for example, to hold the "culture" in each

state constant, and this no doubt has an impact on the giving behavior in each place. However, my estimates should allow us to conclude that welfare spending increases have *some* negative impact on the tendency to give.

14. Leslie Lenkowsky, "Philanthropy and the Welfare State," in *To Empower People: From State to Civil Society*, ed. Michael Novak (Washington, D.C.: American Enterprise Institute Press, 1996), 86.

15. Sam Roberts and Jim Rutenberg, "With More Private Giving, Bloomberg Forges Ties," *New York Times*, May 23, 2005.

16. Source: 2004 Maxwell Poll.

17. Source: 2000, 2002 ANES.

18. For a survey that explains this point, see Bruno S. Frey and Alois Stutzer, "What Can Economists Learn from Happiness Research?" *Journal of Economic Literature* 40, no. 2 (2002): 402–435.

19. Quoted in Waldemar A. Nielsen, *The Big Foundations* (New York: Columbia University Press, 1972), 311.

20. Robert Reich, "Philanthropy and Its Uneasy Relation to Equality," in *Beyond Good Intentions: Learning to Do Good, Not Harm, in Philanthropy*, ed. William Damon and Susan Verducci (Bloomington: Indiana University Press, forthcoming); Richard B. Gunderman, "Giving and Human Excellence: The Paradigm of Liberal Philanthropy" (working paper no. 9, The Philanthropic Enterprise, 2003); Neil Levy, "Against Philanthropy," *Business and Professional Ethics Journal* 21 no. 3–4 (2003): 95–108.

21. David Wagner, *What's Love Got to Do with It? A Critical Look at American Charity* (New York: New Press, 2000), 5. Similarly, the sociologist Janet Poppendieck writes, "By harnessing a wealth of volunteer effort and donations, [food aid to the hungry] makes private programs appear cheaper and more cost effective than their public counterparts, thus reinforcing an ideology of voluntarism that obscures the fundamental destruction of rights." This belief goes far beyond neglecting charity due to a belief in redistribution; rather, it sets the two forces in opposition to one another, and seeks to undermine "voluntarism" to protect "rights." Janet Poppendieck, *Sweet charity? Emergency Food and the End of Entitlement* (New York: Penguin, 1998), 6.

22. From E. C. Lagemann, *The Politics of Knowledge: The Carnegie Corporation, Philanthropy, and Public Policy* (Middletown, Conn.: Wesleyan University Press, 1989), 23–24.

23. Source: 2004 Maxwell Poll.

24. Ibid.

25. Cristopher Graff, "Socialist Leads U.S. Senate Race in Vt.," Associated Press, May 29, 2005, http://abcnews.go.com/Politics/wireStory?id=801422 (accessed March 26, 2006).

26. Andrew Carnegie, "Wealth," *North American Review* CXLVII (June 1889).

27. Herbert Spencer, "Progess: Its Law and Causes," *Westminster Review,* no. 67 (April 1857): 445–485. See also Robert C. Bannister, "William Graham Sumner's 'Social Darwinism' Reconsidered," *History of Political Economy* 5 (1973): 89–109.

28. Margaret Sanger, *Woman and the New Race* (New York: Brentano's, 1920), chap. 18.

29. Brian Micklethwait, "Against Charity: Charity, Favours, Trade and the Welfare State," *Economic Notes* 40 (1992), http://www.libertarian.co.uk/lapubs/econn/econn040.htm (accessed March 26, 2006).

30. Ibid. The left and right seem particularly similar when Micklethwait describes philanthropy as the wealthy "salving their unthinking consciences by chucking gold coins out of their carriages."

31. Thomas Frank, "Why They Won," *New York Times,* November 5, 2004.

32. For the evidence on this point, see Michael J. Graetz and Ian Shapiro, *Death by a Thousand Cuts: The Fight Over Taxing Inherited Wealth* (Princeton, N.J.: Princeton University Press, 2005).

Chapter Four

1. Erich Fromm, *The Art of Loving* (New York: Harper Perennial, 2000), 22.

2. Emily M. Hall, "Profiles in Philanthropy" (Indianapolis: Indiana University Center on Philanthropy, 2003) (see www.learningtogive.org.); Joy Bennett Kinnon, "Factory Worker Gives $700,000 to Charity: Matel Dawson Jr. Contributes to Colleges and Churches," *Ebony,* October 1, 1996.

3. Source: 2000 SCCBS. Mary O'Herlihy, John Havens, and Paul Schervish, "Charitable Giving: How Much, by Whom, and to What?" in *The Nonprofit Sector: A Research Handbook,* 2nd ed., ed. Walter W. Powell and Richard S. Steinberg (New Haven: Yale University Press, forthcoming).

4. Richard Steinberg, "Overall Evaluation of Economic Theories," *Voluntas* 8, no. 2 (1997): 179–204. The exception to the rule that people buy

more items when they earn more is that of what economists call "inferior goods." This does not refer to quality but rather the characteristic that people substitute away from certain things, such as bus travel or Laundromat services, when they become more prosperous. This is not so with charitable giving, though. For a survey on income effects on charity, see Robert McClelland and Arthur C. Brooks, "Comparing Theory and Evidence on the Relationship Between Income and Charitable Giving," *Public Finance Review* 32, no. 5 (2004): 483–497.

5. Source: Giving USA 2005. For an estimate of wealth effects, see McClelland and Brooks, "Comparing Theory and Evidence"; see also Chris Isidore, "The Zero-Savings Problem," *CNNMoney.com*, http://money.cnn.com/2005/08/02/news/economy/savings/ (accessed May 11, 2006).

6. Source: 2000 SCCBS. For more on the "culture of elite philanthropy," see Francie Ostrower, *Why the Wealthy Give: The Culture of Elite Philanthropy* (Princeton, N.J.: Princeton University Press, 1997).

7. Arthur C. Brooks, "Faith, Secularism, and Charity," *Faith and Economics*, no. 43 (2004): 1–8.

8. David M. Van Slyke and Arthur C. Brooks, "Why Do People Give? New Evidence and Strategies for Nonprofit Managers," *American Review of Public Administration* 35, no. 3 (2005): 199–222.

9. McClelland and Brooks, "Comparing Theory and Evidence," 483–497.

10. Source: 2000 SCCBS.

11. Source: 2003 PSID. These calculations do not include nonmoney aid, such as food stamps and public housing.

12. Although there is commonly a racial distinction between working poor (who are largely white) and nonworking poor (disproportionately black) families, race is not the explanation for the difference in charity, and it should not be regarded as any kind of proxy for giving. Indeed, if we look only at the black families in 2003, those not on welfare were nearly three times as likely to give money each year as those on welfare (and two and a half times as likely to give to religious organizations). The charity differences among the poor revolve around welfare, not race.

13. Arthur C. Brooks, "Welfare Receipt and Private Charity," *Public Budgeting and Finance* 22, no. 3 (2002): 100–113; Arthur C. Brooks, "The Effects of Income Redistribution on Giving Behavior" (unpublished manuscript, Syracuse University, Syracuse, New York, 2006).

14. As historian Gertrude Himmelfarb put it, "The Great Society . . . all too often drew [the poor] into a closed society of chronic dependency." Gertrude Himmelfarb, *One Nation, Two Cultures* (New York: Vintage, 2001), 19; source: American Psychological Association, "Making 'Welfare to Work' Really Work," Public Interest Directorate, http://www.apa.org/pi/wpo/myths.html (accessed April 4, 2006).

15. Thomas Jefferson, *Notes on the State of Virginia*, ed. Frank Shuffelton (New York: Penguin Books, 1999); Franklin D. Roosevelt, "Annual Message to Congress," January 4, 1935, in *The Public Papers and Addresses of Franklin D. Roosevelt*, vol. 4, *The Court Disapproves*, 1935, ed. Samuel Rosenman (New York: Random House, 1938). Carter is quoted in Roger A. Freeman, *Does America Neglect Its Poor?* (Stanford, Calif.: The Hoover Institution, 1987), 12.

16. See Richard Wertheimer, Melissa Long, and Sharon Vandivere, "Welfare Recipients' Attitudes Toward Welfare, Nonmarital Childbearing, and Work," paper series B, New Federalism: National Survey of America's Families, no. B–37 (Washington, D.C.: Urban Institute, 2001). According to the economist William Niskanen, "Welfare would provoke little controversy and benefits would probably be higher if these conditions were substantially accidental or temporary—the result, for example, of the death, disability, or temporary unemployment of the major contributor to a family's income. . . . The moral dilemma, of course, is that welfare, like most forms of social insurance, increases the number of people with the insured condition." William Niskanen, "Welfare and the Culture of Poverty," *CATO Journal* 16, no. 1 (1996), http://www.urban.org/publications/310300.html (accessed April 1, 2006).

17. Lawrence M. Mead, *The New Politics of Poverty: The Nonworking Poor in America* (New York: Basic Books, 1992).

18. William Julius Wilson, *The Truly Disadvantaged* (Chicago: University of Chicago Press, 1987).

19. Kathryn Edin and Laura Lein, *Making Ends Meet: How Single Mothers Survive Welfare and Low-Wage Work* (New York: Russell Sage Foundation, 1987).

20. Brooks, "Welfare Receipt and Private Charity," 100–113.

21. The legislation to reform welfare was the Personal Responsibility and Work Opportunity Reconciliation Act of 1996 (PRWORA). The government no longer required recipients to be unmarried and unemployed—on the

contrary, people had to work to receive benefits, if at all possible. The reforms also substituted a system in which 80 percent of support had been dispersed in checks to recipients, with one in which about 60 percent of funds went directly to providing needed services. The most prominent changes, however, were the time limits placed on recipients. All states adopted a five-year lifetime limit on welfare support, and many states also imposed shorter limits on periods of continuous support. The main welfare program's name changed to reflect these limits, from Aid to Families with Dependent Children (AFDC) to Temporary Aid to Needy Families (TANF).

22. Children's Defense Fund, "Edelman Decries President's Betrayal of Promise 'Not to Hurt Children'" (July 31, 1996); Center on Budget and Policy Priorities, "Urban Institute Study Confirms that Welfare Bills Would Increase Child Poverty" (1996), http://www.cbpp.org/URBAN726.HTM.

23. U.S. Bureau of the Census, "Poverty in the United States 1999," http://www.census.gov/prod/2000pubs/p60–210.pdf; Income, Poverty, and Health Insurance Coverage 2003, http://www.whitehouse.gov/infocus/welfarereform; John J. DiIulio Jr., "Older & Wiser?" *Weekly Standard* 11, no. 1 (2005).

24. Source: 2001 PSID, 2003 PSID.

25. Ibid.

26. InnerChange Freedom Initiative, "About IFI Program," http://www.ifiprison.org/channelroot/home/aboutprogram.htm (accessed April 4, 2006).

27. As the White House Web site declares, "President George W. Bush's Faith-Based and Community Initiative represents a fresh start and bold new approach to government's role in helping those in need. Too often the government has ignored or impeded the efforts of faith-based and community organizations. Their compassionate efforts to improve their communities have been needlessly and improperly inhibited by bureaucratic red tape and restrictions placed on funding." White House, "Faith-Based and Community Investment," http://www.whitehouse.gov/infocus/faith-based/ (accessed April 1, 2006); Rickie Solinger, ". . . But No Faith in the People," *Social Justice* 28, no. 1 (2001): 11–13.

28. One author in the magazine the *American Prospect* writes, "A shift out of poverty can only come with a better income-based safety net, higher minimum wages, lower unemployment, fairer tax policies, more refundable tax credits, more unions, better safeguards against discrimination, and other such

progressive policies." Jared Bernstein, "Savings Incentives for the Poor," *American Prospect* 14, no. 5 (2003): A14.

29. Source: 1986 GSS. The estimates here rely on a probit model of the likelihood of saying one is politically conservative, where the independent variables are welfare receipt, religious beliefs, income, education level, gender, marital status, and race.

30. Irving Kristol is often quoted as defining a "neoconservative" as a "liberal who has been mugged by reality." Perhaps stealing a liberal's wallet is a physical application of Kristol's principle.

31. Charles Murray says this about welfare: "The chief defect of the welfare state . . . is not that it is ineffectual in making good on its promises (though it is), nor even that it often exacerbates the very problems it is supposed to solve (though it does). The welfare state is pernicious ultimately because it drains too much of the life from life." Nowhere is this statement truer, it seems, than the life people can experience in compassion and voluntary charity. Charles Murray, "A Plan to Replace the Welfare State," *Wall Street Journal,* March 22, 2006, A16.

32. Robert E. Rector, "Means-Tested Welfare Spending: Past and Future Growth," *Heritage Foundation,* 2001; Sources: 2003 PSID, 2000 GVS; Mother Theresa, *A Gift for God* (New York: HarperCollins, 1976).

33. James Q. Wilson, *The Marriage Problem: How Our Culture Has Weakened Families* (New York: HarperCollins, 2002); Victoria L. Brown, Isaac D. Montoya, and Cheryl A. Dayton-Shotts, "Trends of Criminal Activity and Substance Use in a Sample of Welfare Recipients," *Crime & Delinquency* 50, no. 1 (2004): 6–23.

Chapter Five

1. This is taken from a discussion between the author and Dianna Smiley (Program Director for Education and Outreach, National Center for Family Philanthropy), June 2005. See also the report *Six Tips on Raising Philanthropic Children,* http://www.ncfp.org/FGN-July_2005/upfront.html.

2. Source: 2000 SCCBS. The model here regresses dollars given annually to charity, and the number of occasions volunteered, on one's family size and the other demographics mentioned. I estimated the model using the tobit procedure.

3. A. Crittenden, *The Price of Motherhood: Why the Most Important Job in the World Is Still the Least Valued* (New York: Metropolitan Books, 2001); R. Lee and T. Miller, Population Policy and Externalities to Childbearing, *Annals of the American Academy of Political and Social Sciences* 510 (1990): 17–43.

4. Source: 2001 GVS. The model here is a probit estimation of the likelihood of volunteering on a dummy variable for parental volunteering as well as the demographics listed. A similar difference exists for strictly informal volunteering.

5. Source: 2001 Giving and Volunteering Survey. Forty-one percent of nonchurch members with volunteer parents volunteered themselves as adults.

6. Mark Wilhelm, Eleanor Brown, Patrick Rooney, and Richard Steinberg, "The Intergenerational Transmission of Generosity," working paper, Indiana University–Purdue University, Indianapolis, 2004. Interestingly, the researchers did not find that, all else held constant, secular giving by parents leads to religious giving by their children, or vice versa.

7. David Lykken and Auke Tellegen, "Happiness Is a Stochastic Phenomenon," *Psychological Science* 7, no. 3 (1996); Thomas J. Bouchard and Matt McGue, "Genetic and Environmental Influences on Human Psychological Differences," *Journal of Neurobiology* 54 (2003): 4–45; Thomas J. Bouchard, "The Genetics of Personality," in *Handbook of Psychiatric Genetics*, ed. K. Blum and E. P. Noble (Boca Raton, Fla.: CRC Press, 1997), 273–296; H. H. Maes et al., "Religious Attendance and Frequency of Alcohol Use: Same Genes or Same Environments: A Bivariate Extended Twin Kinship Model," *Twin Res* 2 (1999): 169–179.

8. According to the American Psychological Association: "Not everyone has time to devote to volunteer work or money to donate to causes" (an assertion that we know is incorrect), "but there are small acts of caring that can be part of your family's life. These acts of caring don't have to be grandiose. Doing a favor for a neighbor, taking a stray animal to a shelter, giving money and a kind word to a homeless person, helping out when a group of teenagers are cruelly teasing a classmate; there are all kinds of small acts of compassion that your children can watch you do, and even take part in themselves." American Psychological Association, "What Makes Kids Care? Teaching Gentleness in a Violent World," http://www.apa.org/pubinfo/altruism.html (accessed April 11, 2006).

9. Source: 2001 PSID. This analysis regresses donations on inherited income, earned income, age, gender, marital status, household size, education,

religious affiliation, and race. I estimate the model using ordinary least squares. The marginal donations are low because most giving is explained by the non-financial variables.

10. Source: 1999 ARS.

11. Ibid. This analysis relies on a probit model that regresses the likelihood of giving on the demographics listed, as well as religious attendance as a child.

12. This is a simple probability model. Note that the woman and her husband each have a 0.5 likelihood of not donating, so—assuming their decisions are independent—together their chance of not donating is $(0.5)(0.5)=0.25$, and thus the likelihood of donating is $1 - 0.25 = 0.75$.

13. Source: 2002 GSS. Marriage, however, can also work against charity. When a team of economists examined how couples actually make decisions about charity, they found that any disagreement about giving tends to push total household giving down; for example, if the newly married woman in the previous example wants to give to her church but her husband prefers to give to the local opera company instead, their compromise will more often than not be to give to *neither*. Single people make decisions on their own, and therefore do not have such conflicts. James Andreoni, Eleanor Brown, and Isaac Rischall, "Charitable Giving by Married Couples: Who Decides and Why Does it Matter?" *Journal of Human Resources* 38, no. 1 (2003): 111–133.

14. Source: 2002 GSS.

15. Ibid. I estimate the probability of giving and volunteering with a probit model, where the different marital statuses and demographic characteristics are on the right-hand side. Married people are more religious and have higher incomes than divorced people, a demographic that best explains the charity differences between married and divorced parents.

16. Council of Economic Advisers, "Inequality and Economic Rewards" in *Economic Report of the President* (Washington, D.C.: U.S. Government Printing Office, 1997), 163–188.

17. James Q. Wilson, *The Marriage Problem: How Our Culture Has Weakened Families* (New York: HarperCollins, 2002).

18. Ibid.

19. According to the psychologist Robert Coles, "In elementary school, maybe as never before or afterward, given favorable family and neighborhood circumstances, the child becomes an intensely moral creature, quite interested in figuring out the reasons of this world: how and why things work, but also,

how and why he or she should behave in various situations." Quoted in Kathryn A. Agard, "Raising Kids Who Give, Share & Care," Learning to Give, http://www.learningtogive.org/parents/raising/ (accessed April 11, 2006).

20. R. E. Emery, *Marriage, Divorce, and Children's Adjustment* (Thousand Oaks, Calif.: Sage, 1999).

21. Source: 2002 GSS.

22. Ibid. A regression (using the tobit specification to take account of the censoring in the number of children) of the number of children an adult has on ideology, religion, marital status, education, age, income, and race yields barely insignificant coefficients on political views. However, these coefficients are negative for liberals and positive for conservatives. Significant effects are religious behavior, age, education, and race.

23. Source: 2002 GSS. Using a probit estimation, I model the likelihood of a respondent's reporting that he or she was "very happy" on a vector of demographics and political views.

24. United for a Fair Economy, "Frequently Asked Questions About the Estate Tax," http://www.faireconomy.org/estatetax/ETFAQ.html (accessed April 11, 2006).

25. Pamela Greene and Robert McClelland, "The Effects of Federal Estate Tax Policy on Charitable Contributions" (technical papers series, Congressional Budget Office, 2001).

26. Paul G. Schervish, "Philanthropy Can Thrive Without Estate Tax," *Chronicle of Philanthropy*, January 11, 2001.

27. Source: 2001 PSID; John J. Havens and Paul G. Schervish, "Millionaires and the Millenium: New Estimates of the Forthcoming Wealth Transfer and the Prospects for a Golden Age of Philanthropy" (working paper, Boston College Social Welfare Research Institute, October 19, 1999).

Chapter Six

1. Matthew Arnold, *Selected Poems and Prose,* ed. Miriam Allot (London: J. M. Dent, 1993).

2. Adam Smith, *The Theory of Moral Sentiments* (Cambridge: Cambridge University Press, 2002), 157.

3. "Helping the Survivors," *Economist,* January 8, 2005.

4. Tsunami aid has been tallied by the Indiana Center on Philanthropy; see http://www.philanthropy.iupui.edu/. Rachel Emma Silverman and

Elizabeth Bernstein, "New Challenge for Aid Groups: Lots of Money," *Wall Street Journal,* January 4, 2005.

5. Rick Cohen, "The Tsunami Tsunami: The Charitable and Political Response to the Disaster," *Nonprofit Quarterly* 11, no. 4 (2004).

6. Jefferson Morley, "Is America Stingy?" *Washington Post,* April 4, 2005.

7. "U.S. 'turning its back' on poverty," *BBC News,* November 20, 2001, http://news.bbc.co.uk/1/hi/uk_politics/1666626.stm (accessed April 20, 2006).

8. Some scholars also count the remittances of private individuals to their families overseas in this number as well, which amounted to another $18 billion in 2000. However, I have omitted this amount because some believe it should not be classified as charitable giving. See USAID, *Foreign Aid in the National Interest: Promoting Freedom, Security, and Opportunity* (Washington, D.C.: USAID, 2002); Carol C. Adelman, "The Privatization of Foreign Aid: Reassessing National Largesse," *Foreign Affairs* 82, no. 6 (2003): 9.

9. Source: Johns Hopkins Comparative Nonprofit Sector Project. See http://www.jhu.edu/cnp (accessed May 17, 2006).

10. Source for purchasing power-corrected 1998 GDP: World Bank; see http://web.worldbank.org/WBSITE/EXTERNAL/DATASTATISTICS/0,, contentMDK:20535285~menuPK:1192694~pagePK:64133150~piPK:64133 175~theSitePK:239419,00.html (accessed May 17, 2006).

11. The only other country that competes with the United States in the Johns Hopkins data is Israel, which gives less per capita, but slightly more when adjusted for income.

12. Source: 1998 International Social Survey Programme (ISSP) (Zentralarchiv für Empirische Sozialforschung). This is an annual survey of about 1,000 citizens in each of about thirty countries around the world, approximately half of which are Western European. Most of the European countries in the ISSP are the same as those from the Hopkins data: The ISSP did not include Belgium or Finland, but did include Cyprus, Northern Ireland, Switzerland, Portugal, Denmark, and Eastern Germany. This analysis pools the data across all sixteen European nations and the United States, and regresses a vector of demographic variables as well as dummy variables for each European nation (leaving the United States as the reference group) on a dummy variable for volunteering. The results reported here come from the marginal effects calculated from a probit estimation.

13. The colleague referred to here is my dear friend Alexander Livshin, professor of public administration at Moscow State University.

14. Organization for Economic Co-operation and Development (OECD), *OECD in Washington*, report no. 42 (Washington, D.C.: OECD, 2003), 1.

15. James Sproule, "International Commentary: Why Are Your Neighbors Paying in Cash?" *Wall Street Journal Europe*, February 28, 2001.

16. François Heisbourg, Director of the Foundation for Strategic Research in Paris, quoted in Adam G. Mersereau, "Casualties of Enlightenment," *National Review*, March 19, 2003; Régis DeBray, "The French Lesson," *New York Times*, February 23, 2003.

17. Source: 2002, 1998 ISSP. The Irish (63 percent of whom reported attending church weekly in 1998) seem to provide a dramatic counterexample to the European secular trend. However, a more likely interpretation is that the Irish simply have not yet caught up with the rest of Europe. One way to illustrate the trend is by looking at religious participation by age group. Among people older than sixty—those raised in a time before Ireland was particularly integrated into Europe—the rate of regular church attendance is 91 percent (compared with "just" 49 percent of Americans older than sixty). For Irish between forty-one and fifty years of age, the churchgoing percentage is 61 percent (versus 32 percent of Americans). But for Irish in their twenties, the rate is just 31 percent—not far from the American rate for that age group of 25 percent.

18. Source: 1998 ISSP. First, I pool approximately 27,000 people in the multicountry European sample, and then regress religious and secular behavior, other relevant sociodemographics, and country-level dummies on the volunteering variables. I use a binary probit model for this estimation, and evaluate the results at their partial derivatives to obtain the marginal effect. Second, I run similar models for specific European countries.

19. Source: 1998 ISSP. Here, I include the United States and France samples, and create dummies for secularist French and religious American. I add the value of the coefficient for each dummy to the average volunteering and nonreligious volunteering rates for the pooled sample.

20. José Casanova, *"Catholic Poland in Post-Christian Europe,"* *Tr@nsit online*, Nr. 25/2003, http://www.iwm.at/index.php?option=com_content&task=view&id=239&Itemid=415 (accessed April 20, 2006); J. H. H. Weiler, *Un'Europa Cristiana* (Milan: Biblioteca Universale Rizzoli, 2003); Pope Benedict XVI, *Christianity and the Crisis of Cultures* (Fort Collins, Colo.: Ignatius Press, 2005).

21. Laurence R. Iannaccone, "Introduction to the Economics of Religion," *Journal of Economic Literature* 36 (1998): 1465–1496. Church membership is generally higher than weekly attendance. For example, in 1999, 61 percent of the population reported belonging to a house of worship, but only 34 percent said they attended at least once a week.

22. Sources: 1996, 1998 ISSP. Respondents were presented with some form of this statement: "The government has a responsibility to reduce income inequality." They were asked to "strongly agree," "agree," "neither agree nor disagree," "disagree," or "strongly disagree." When I talk about the population percentage's agreeing, I am referring to people in the first two categories. This analysis employs an ordinary least squares model in which average volunteering level from each country in 1996 is regressed on average agreement with income redistribution in 1998.

23. Derek Jeffers and Elisabeth Sanguinetti, "France: Rightist Le Pen Gains Strength," *The Militant* 60, no. 38 (1996).

24. Micael J. Sodaro, "Whatever Happened to Eurocommunism?" *Problems of Communism* 33, no. 4 (1984): 59–65; Robert Kagan, "Power and Weakness," *Policy Review* 113, no. 3 (2002).

25. Robert J. Samuelson, "The End of Europe," *Washington Post,* June 15, 2005, A25; Brendan Conway, "Europe Today," *Washington Times,* July 24, 2005; George Weigel, *The Cube and the Cathedral* (New York: Basic Books, 2005), 22.

26. Source: U.S. Census, Population Division, International Programs Center. The 2000 EU birthrate was similar to the rate of 1.64 children per woman in non-EU European countries. Patrick Festy, "Looking for European Demography, Desperately?" Population Division, Department of Economic and Social Affairs, United Nations, http://www.un.org/esa/population/publications/popdecline/festy.pdf (accessed May 1, 2006); "The Fertility Bust," *Economist,* February 9, 2006.

27. Festy, "Looking for European Demography, Desperately?"; *Agence France Presse,* "Marriage on the Rocks in Britain," September 30, 2005.

28. Source: 2002 ISSP.

29. Günter Grass, *Headbirths: Or The Germans Are Dying Out* (Fort Washington, Pa.: Harvest Books Reprints (1990 [1982])).

30. Using the 1998 ISSP data, I regress a dummy for annual family volunteering on household size and the demographics mentioned; I use a probit model and acquire the marginal effects from each regressor. The

marginal effect of an extra household member was 6 percentage points (so two kids would push up the likelihood of volunteering by approximately 12 points), and the population proportion volunteering was 0.37.

31. Rand Corporation, "Population Implosion? Low Fertility and Policy Responses in the European Union," RAND research brief, RB–9126-EC, 2004.

32. Organization for Economic Co-operation and Development (OECD), *Main Economic Indicators* (Washington, D.C.: OECD, 2005); Fareed Zakaria, "The Decline and Fall of Europe," *Newsweek,* February 20, 2006; Fulcrum Financial Inquiry, "Europe's Self-Inflicted Economic Injuries," http://www.fulcruminquiry.com, 2005; Fredrik Berström and Robert Gidehag, *EU Versus USA* (Stockholm: Timbro, 2004).

33. 2002 ISSP.

Chapter Seven

1. Peter Collier and David Horowitz, *The Rockefellers, an American Dynasty* (New York: Holt, Rinehart and Winston, 1976), 48.

2. See Soma Hewa, "The Protestant Ethic and Rockefeller Benevolence: The Religious Impulse in American Philanthropy," *Journal for the Theory of Social Behavior* 27, no. 4 (1997): 419–452.

3. Quoted in Hewa, 428.

4. John Bunyan, *The Pilgrim's Progress,* ed. Charles Eliot, vol. 15, pt. 1, *The Harvard Classics* (New York: P. F. Collier and Son, 1909–1914), 521–522.

5. Arthur C. Brooks, *Social Entrepreneurship: A Modern Approach to Social Value Creation* (Upper Saddle River, N.J.: Prentice-Hall, forthcoming 2007).

6. Robert D. Putnam, *Bowling Alone: The Collapse and Revival of American Community* (New York: Simon and Schuster, 2000). Putnam distinguishes charitable acts from other kinds of civic engagement, such as engaging in community activities, because the latter are "doing with," the former "doing for." Nonetheless, he notes their similarity.

7. George Gilder, "The Moral Sources of Capitalism," in *The Essential Neoconservative Reader,* ed. Mark Gerson (Reading, Mass.: Addison-Wesley, 1996), 155, 157.

8. Thorstein Veblen, "Survivals of the Non-Invidious Interest," in *The Theory of the Leisure Class: An Economic Study of Institutions* (New York: The Macmillan Company, 1899), 334; William Shakespeare, "Pericles, Prince of

Tyre," in *The Complete Works of William Shakespeare,* ed. W. J. Craig (London: Oxford University Press, 1914; *Bartleby.com,* 2000), http://www.bartleby.com/70/ (accessed May 1, 2006).

9. See A. Bandura, "Self-Efficacy," in *Encyclopedia of Human Behavior,* ed. V. S. Ramachaudran (New York: Academic Press, 1994), 4:71–81.

10. Victor Frankl, *Man's Search for Meaning* (New York: Pocket Books, 1984), 133.

11. Proverbs 11:24. Matthew Henry, *Commentary: On the Whole Bible,* http://www.ccel.org/h/henry/mhc2/MHC20011.HTM (accessed April 20, 2006). The full passage: "It is possible a man may grow rich by prudently spending what he has, may scatter in works of piety, charity, and generosity, and yet may increase; nay, by that means may increase, as the corn is increased by being sown. By cheerfully using what we have our spirits are exhilarated, and so fitted for the business we have to do, by minding which closely what we have is increased; it gains a reputation which contributes to the increase. But it is especially to be ascribed to God; he blesses the giving hand, and so makes it a getting hand." The Dalai Lama is quoted in Richard Layard, *Happiness: Lessons from a New Science* (New York: Penguin Press, 2005), 190.

12. Source: 2000 SCCBS. The model described here uses ordinary least squares (OLS) to estimate the effects on household income of giving and volunteering plus the demographics listed.

13. This conclusion is the product of a two-stage least squares regression in which income is regressed on a vector of demographics and a fitted value of charitable donations. This fitted value comes from a regression of donations on volunteer time plus appropriate demographics. Volunteer time meets the criteria for a high-quality instrument in this system. The result is robust to specification; for example, a full-information maximum likelihood tobit model (to take account of the censoring in giving) produces a marginal giving effect of $3.89.

14. Data in this discussion come from the Statistical Abstract of the United States (various years), and historical giving data from Indiana University's Center on Philanthropy. I infer causality through the use of Granger tests, in which I regress real GDP per capita on current real giving per capita, three annual lagged values of giving, and three annual lags in GDP. I do the same for a model regressing donations on lagged values of giving and lagged values of GDP. I run models with logged and nonlogged values to estimate elasticities and marginal dollar effects (the elasticities are detailed in the appendix), and use chi-square hypothesis tests in an attempt to reject the

hypotheses that each dependent variable is not associated with the lags in itself and the lags in the other variable. In all cases, the chi-square measures are sufficiently large to reject the hypotheses that the variables are unrelated. Most notably, the hypothesis that GDP per capita is unrelated to the current and lagged values of average giving produces a test statistic of 4.92 with 40 degrees of freedom, meaning that the hypothesis can be rejected at the 0.001 level.

15. Sources: Johns Hopkins Comparative Nonprofit Sector Project, http://www.jhu.edu/cnp (accessed May 17, 2006); 1998 ISSP.

16. Irving Kristol, "A Conservative Welfare State," *Wall Street Journal*, June 14, 1993.

17. Intuition here might be mixed. It is well-known that people providing help to others—especially sick family members—can suffer physical and mental health ill-effects. For example, researchers have found that fully a third of primary caregivers for demented family members suffer from clinical depression. This has often been interpreted as evidence that giving care can make you sick, although this interpretation is probably incorrect. A recent study of caregivers of severely disabled relatives found that it was *needs* of the disabled—not the caregiving itself—that led to the ill-effects on the caregivers. See Anna A. Amirkhanyan and Douglas A. Wolf, "Caregiver Stress and Noncaregiver Stress: Exploring the Pathways of Psychiatric Morbidity," *Gerentologist* 43, no. 6 (2003): 817–827.

18. Source: 2000 SCCBS. Kenneth E. Covinsky et al., "Patient and Caregiver Characteristics Associated with Depression in Caregivers of Patients with Dementia," *Journal of General Internal Medicine* 18, no. 12 (2003): 1006–1014.

19. Source 2000 SCCBS. The analysis here relies on probit regressions, where the dependent variables are "excellent" health, and a response of "very happy." The independent variables are binary measures of giving and volunteering, as well as the demographics listed.

20. Source: 2002 GSS. The analysis here relies on probit regressions, where the dependent variable is someone reporting that he or she is "very happy." The population is limited to those reporting excellent health; the independent variables are binary measures of giving blood annually, as well as the demographics listed.

21. Alex H. Harris and Carl E. Thoresen, "Volunteering Is Associated with Delayed Mortality in Older People: Analysis of the Longitudinal Study of Aging," *Journal of Health Psychology* 10, no. 6 (2005): 739–752.

22. Carolyn E. Schwartz and Rabbi Meir Sendor, "Helping Others Helps Oneself: Response Shift Effects in Peer Support," *Social Science and Medicine* 48 (1999): 1563–1575. In this study, the treatment group was assigned to provide "compassionate, unconditional positive regard" for others with the same chronic disease—that is, they were asked to provide a sympathetic ear—to the members of the control group.

23. Carolyn Schwartz et al., "Altruistic Social Interest Behaviors Are Associated with Better Mental Health," *Psychosomatic Medicine* 65 (2003): 778–785. Carey Goldberg, "For Good Health, It Is Better to Give, Science Suggests," *Boston Globe*, November 28, 2003; Allan Luks and Ellen Payne, *The Healing Power of Doing Good: The Health and Spiritual Benefits of Helping Others* (New York: Fawcett Columbine, 1991); Paul Pearsall, *The Pleasure Prescription: To Love, to Work, to Play—Life in the Balance* (Alameda, Calif.: Hunter House, 1996).

24. Alexis de Tocqueville, *Democracy in America,* ed. J. P. Maier, trans. George Lawrence (Garden City, N.Y.: Anchor Books, 1969).

25. Peter L. Berger and Richard John Neuhaus, *To Empower People: From State to Civil Society* (Washington, D.C.: AEI Press, 1996 [1977]), 189.

26. Perhaps, by incorporating these institutions into our governance, we have redefined government itself, driving us toward Thomas Jefferson's vision of "making every citizen an acting member of the government, and in the offices nearest and most interesting to him, will attach him by his strongest feelings to the independence of his country, and its republican constitution." Thomas Jefferson to Samuel Kercheval, July 12, 1816, in *The Writings of Thomas Jefferson,* ed. A. Lipscomb and A. E. Bergh (memorial edition) (Washington, D.C.: Thomas Jefferson Memorial Association, 1903–1904), 15:37.

27. Sources: 2000 SCCBS, 2004 Maxwell Poll.

28. Leslie Lenkowsky, "Can Government Build Community? Lessons from the National Service Program," in *Gifts of Time and Money: The Role of Charity in America's Communities,* ed. Arthur C. Brooks (Lanham, Md.: Rowman and Littlefield, 2005), 11–31.

29. Ibid., 13.

30. Arthur M. Okun, *Equality and Efficiency: The Big Tradeoff* (Washington, D.C.: Brookings Institution Press, 1975).

31. David Callahan, *The Cheating Culture* (Orlando, Fla.: Harcourt, 2004).

32. See Robert H. Frank, *Luxury Fever: Money and Happiness in an Era of Excess* (Princeton, N.J.: Princeton University Press, 2000).

Chapter Eight

1. Essayist Joseph Epstein told this story at the American Enterprise Institute Bradley Lecture, April 15, 1996.

2. John Stossel, "Big Government Discourages Private Charity," *Real Clear Politics,* August 24, 2005. Technically, of course, Jesus Christ ran into considerably *more* trouble with the government than the San Francisco drug rehabilitation clinic.

3. New Jersey Office of Recreation, http://www.state.nj.us/dca/rec/sport.

4. Eric Brunner and Jennifer Imazeki, "Private Contributions and Public School Resources," working paper no. 07–03, San Diego State University Department of Economics, San Diego, California, 2003.

5. Rhode Island General Laws § 11–56–1 (1994).

6. T. E. McCollough, *Truth and Ethics in School Reform* (Washington, D.C.: Council for Educational Development and Research, 1992).

7. Robert Cooter and Brian J. Broughman, "Charity, Publicity, and the Donation Registry," *Economists' Voice* 2, no. 3 (2005).

8. Eleanor Brown and Al Slivinski, "Nonprofit Organizations and the Market," in *The Nonprofit Sector: A Research Handbook,* ed. Walter Powell and Richard Steinberg (New Haven, Conn.: Yale University Press, forthcoming).

9. Arthur C. Brooks, "In Search of True Public Arts Support," *Public Budgeting & Finance* 24, no. 2, (2004): 88–100; Michael Rushton and Arthur C. Brooks, "Government Funding of Nonprofit Organizations," in *An Integrated Theory of Nonprofit Finance,* ed. Dennis R. Young (Lanham, Md.: Lexington Books, forthcoming).

10. Source: 2001 PSID. People who do not itemize their deductions still receive the standard deduction (in the United States), but this does not compensate them for their charitable giving. Arthur C. Brooks, "Why Museums Trump Churches," *Wall Street Journal,* April 15, 2005, A10.

11. This last idea is described in Aaron S. Edlin, "The Choose-your-Charity Tax: A Way to Incentivize Greater Giving," *Economists' Voice* 2, no. 3 (2005).

12. See http://www.commoncents.org.

13. These data came from an internal survey provided to the author by Common Cents.

14. See http://www.cnycf.org/pieproject/.

15. Arthur C. Brooks, "The Effects of Public Policy on Private Charity," *Administration & Society* 36, no. 2 (2004): 166–185; Independent Sector, *The New Nonprofit Almanac in Brief* (Washington D.C.: Independent Sector, 2001), www.IndependentSector.org.

16. Arthur C. Brooks, "What Do Nonprofit Organizations Seek? (And Why Should Policymakers Care?)" *Journal of Policy Analysis and Management* 24, no. 3 (2005): 543–558.

17. Carrie A. Moore, "Wealth & Faith: The More Philanthropists Give, the More They Enjoy Giving," *Deseret News,* May 3, 2003; Jeff Brooks, "Donor Power: How to Meet the New Generation of Donors," *Loyalty* (newsletter of Merkle-Domain), 2004.

18. These data come from proprietary fund-raising data; the findings are consistent with those of other studies.

19. James Andreoni and Abigail Payne, "Do Government Grants to Private Charities Crowd Out Giving or Fundraising?" *American Economic Review* 93, no. 3 (June 2003): 792–812.

20. See http://www.charitynavigator.org/index.cfm/bay/content.view/catid/2/cpid/48.htm.

21. Quoted in Gertrude Himmelfarb, *One Nation, Two Cultures* (New York: Vintage, 2001), 157.

22. Sources: The Pew Research Center for the People and the Press, "Religion: A Strength and Weakness for Both Parties," http://www.people-press.org (2005); 1972–1998 GSS; Stephen Carter, *The Dissent of the Governed: A Meditation on Law, Religion, and Loyalty* (Cambridge, Mass.: Harvard University Press, 1998), 9.

23. Joseph Loconte, "Nearer, My God, to the G.O.P.," *New York Times,* January 2, 2006.

24. Morris Berman, *The Twilight of American Culture* (New York: Norton, 2001), 33; Tony Hendra, "The Cheney Files," *American Prospect,* August 17, 2004, http://www.prospect.org/web/page.ww?section=root&name=ViewWeb &articleId=8365 (accessed May 31, 2006).

Appendix

1. Arthur C. Brooks, "What Do 'Don't Know' Responses Really Mean in Giving Surveys?" *Nonprofit and Voluntary Sector Quarterly* 33, no. 3 (2004): 423–434.

2. Clive W. J. Granger, "Investigating Causal Relations by Econometric Models and Cross-Spectral Methods," *Econometrica* 37, no. 3 (1969): 424–438.

3. See http://poll.campbellinstitute.org.

4. Kathy S. Steinberg and Patrick M. Rooney, "America Gives: A Survey of Americans' Generosity After September 11," *Nonprofit and Voluntary Sector Quarterly* 34, no. 1 (2005): 110–135.

Acknowledgments

Writing a book can be an exercise in emotional fortitude. As a manuscript gestates, an author's need for honest criticism grows in inverse proportion to his ability to forbear that criticism. In the case of *Who Really Cares*, I am indebted to the people who knew this and delicately told me the truth anyway. This book is far better than it would have been without their input.

James Q. Wilson read the whole manuscript as I was writing it, and saw my earliest drafts. My writing was always much rougher than his criticisms, and I am deeply grateful for his careful and thoughtful guidance. Rogan Kersh not only read the book but also suggested the title. Peter Schuck and David Mustard also read the entire manuscript, giving me exceptionally helpful suggestions. This project wouldn't have gotten started at all, were it not for Leslie Lenkowsky, whose mentorship helped me understand how the basic ideas might become a book.

Many other people read chapters and sections, and helped me brainstorm ideas. These people include Scott Allard, Stephen Bowman, Allison Brooks, Jeff Brooks, Peter Frumkin, Henry Givray, Gary Lavine, Jill Leonhardt, Mel Levitsky, Alexander Livshin, Joe Loconte, Len Lopoo, Steve Lux, Keith McAllister,

Megan McAllister, Ram Mohan Mishra, Henry Olsen, Jeff Straussman, David Van Slyke, Scott Walter, Barry Weiss, Doug Wolf, and Adam Wolfson. For suggestions leading to changes in the paperback edition of *Who Really Cares,* I am grateful to Michael Medved, Greg Margolin, and Andrew Moravcsik.

This book project received generous support from the Earhart Foundation and the Achelis & Bodman Foundations. These foundations and their executives—Montgomery Brown, Bruce Frohnen, Joseph Dolan, and John Krieger—continue the truly progressive philanthropic tradition of supporting the development of good ideas—and I am honored that they placed my ideas in this category. Two generous individuals who also supported this project were Judith Greenberg Seinfeld and Gary Lavine. The institutional support I received from the Maxwell School and the Campbell Public Affairs Institute was critical to the success of the book, and I am grateful for this. The school also provided direct support in the form of an Appleby-Mosher Grant to purchase data used in the analysis, and funded my research assistant, Annie Ju.

My editor at Basic Books, Lara Heimert, is not only a brilliant and creative editor, but also understands the delicate psyche of an author in the middle of a book. Her unfailing optimism and enthusiasm made the editing process not just painless, but an authentically enjoyable experience. I received outstanding suggestions and assistance from others at Basic as well, including David Steinberger, John Sherer, Kay Mariea, Jennifer Blakebrough-Raeburn, Michele Jacob, Julie McCarroll, and Nikil Saval.

I am grateful to Lisa Adams, my agent at the Garamond Agency, who took a chance on what was an unwritten book, helped me make the idea into something attractive to publishers, gave me valuable comments on various drafts, and injected sense into the whole project.

ACKNOWLEDGMENTS

I had the opportunity to develop many of the ideas in this book in the pages of the *Wall Street Journal* and *CBSnews.com*. I have the op-ed editors of each, Tunku Varadarajan and Dick Meyer, to thank for that. Other journals, newspapers, and magazines that published ideas I ultimately used in this book are *The Public Interest*, *Policy Review*, *Philanthropy*, the *Chronicle of Philanthropy*, *Journal of Policy Analysis and Management*, *Public Administration Review*, and *Public Budgeting and Finance*.

The data for this book came from a lot of sources over the years. Much of it is publicly available from the Inter-University Consortium for Political and Social Research, the Roper Center for Public Opinion Research, and the University of Michigan. Patrick Rooney and Kathy Steinberg provided me with the *America Gives* survey data, and Melissa Brown shared data on aggregate American philanthropy over the past half century. In addition, many practitioners in the field of philanthropy helped me to make sense of my findings, and gave me important background information. These people included Kim Scott of the Central New York Community Foundation, Adam Seidel of Common Cents, Stephanie Judson from the South Dakota Community Foundation, Dianna Smiley from the National Center for Family Philanthropy, Dr. Ronald Saletsky from Upstate Medical University, Gustav Niebuhr from Syracuse University, and Kathryn Agard from Learning to Give.

Finally, I would not have written this book without the collaboration of my intellectual co-conspirator and wife, Ester Munt-Brooks, to whom this book is dedicated. She had a hand in the development of all the ideas and worked with me through version after painful version of the manuscript. I am also grateful to our children, Quimet, Carlos, and Marina, who show me every day how to be more charitable, and why charity matters.

Index